"Hail glorious St. Patrick
dear saint of our isle
on us thy poor children
bestow a sweet smile,
and now thou art high
in the mansion above
on Erin's green valleys
look down with thy love."

A Child's Hymn to St. Patrick

MJF dba Educare
Santa Clara, California

"*I endorse* The Definitive St. Patrick's Day Festivity Book. *We are all acquainted with St. Patrick's Day celebrations, but this book puts them in both Material and Spiritual perspective. It is important to not just celebrate Ireland and its people, but also to understand its history and culture.*"

—Rev. Theodore M. Hesburgh, C.S.C.,
President Emeritus, University of Notre Dame, Indiana

"*A 'pot o' gold' of Irish wit, blessings, proverbs, laments; a must for the planner of a St. Patrick's Day gathering!*"

—Barry Reed, Attorney at Law, Author,
The Verdict, The Choice, The Indictment; Boston, MA

" *I found [Michael Fallon's] book to be as rewarding as [Irish potatoes] and corned beef & cabbage. This is more than a mere 'How-to-Party' book; it is more a celebration of the Irish at their fun-loving best. "There are games —some centuries old— filled with nostalgic memories.*

"You hear the tapping of feet dancing a traditional Irish 'jig' —the songs of a proud and sentimental people— and the wit and humor that evoke smiles in all of us, Irish or not!

"Through it all, Saint Patrick himself comes alive as a personable human being, eminently likable, but presented with due reverence. The Definitive St. Patrick's Day Festivity Book *has accomplished its purpose!***"**

—HENRY D. SPALDING, Author,
The Joys of Irish Humor; Los Angeles, CA

"*Whether Irish, American-Irish, or just 'Irish-at-Heart,' people do want to celebrate St. Patrick's Day —or days. In our neck-of-the-woods, [St. Patrick's Day] may last all March! In our fast moving society of today, it's good to take time to remember the past, visit with friends, and share.* The Definitive St. Patrick's Day Festivity Book *has many options. It gives many ideas —from singing to toasting. May it spark an idea or two to the reader in wishing 'all the warmest St. Patrick's Day.'"*

—JOHN HANNEGAN, Irish Restaurateur, President, San Jose-Dublin Sister City Program, Los Gatos, CA

"The Definitive St. Patrick's Day Festivity Book *captures the light-hearted side of the Irish mystic. Its short compendium of Gaelic anecdotes and celebrations remind us all of the wealth of humor that is so much a part of the culture. I found Michael Fallon's volume to be informative and refreshing. This book is certainly a coffee-table special for its quick glimpses into Irish ways."*

—JEREMY P. ROCHE, Educator, President,
Irish Children's Fund, Inc., Chicago, IL

"A most entertaining book. It belongs on the bookshelf of every man or woman that loves the spoken or written word. It can arm your mind with a quip, a witticism or anecdote that you wished you had at the given time when you knew not the day nor the hour you needed it. Thank you, Michael, for The Definitive St. Patrick's Day Festivity Book. *It is a treasure —a grand tribute to a grand day!"*

—SHAY DUFFIN, Actor, *The Leprechaun,*
Author, Playwright, *Brendan Behan,* Redondo Beach, CA

"Speaking as a descendant of Tipperary, Cork and Kerry —with a Norman mother and an Irish father— I recommend Michael James Fallon's handy The Definitive St. Patrick's Day Festivity Book."

—REV. GEORGE R. SULLIVAN, SJ.,
Vice President, Gregorian University Foundation,
Los Angeles, CA

"I found this book to be novel and unique. It should appeal to a wide audience, Irish or otherwise, in their planning and celebrating St. Patrick's Day. This book is a resource that should be kept on a nearby shelf for easy reference to its proverbs, blessings and toasts; or to take one back in time to Ireland herself. Joyfully reading its pages, I thought of my own years growing up in Ireland...."

—RAY O'FLAHERTY,
Consultant, Industrial Development Board for Northern Ireland;
Vice-President, Levart Travel Services, San Jose, CA

The Definitive
St. Patrick's Day
Festivity Book

*Enhance the Celebration
of the Irish in us all*

The Definitive St. Patrick's Day Festivity Book

by
Michael James Fallon

MJF dba Educare
Santa Clara, California
1997

MJF dba Educare
1114 Pomeroy Avenue
Santa Clara, California 95051

Educare books are available at
special discounts for bulk purchases for sales promotions,
premiums, fund raising, or educational use.
For details contact: Educare

THE DEFINITIVE ST. PATRICK'S DAY FESTIVITY BOOK
ISBN - 0 9660687-0-X

Library of Congress Catalog Card Number: 97-76689

Publisher's Cataloging-in-Publication
(Prepared by Quality Books, Inc.)

Fallon, Michael J.
        The Definitive St. Patrick's Day Festivity Book
        / by Michael J. Fallon
        p. cm.
        Includes biographical references
        1. St. Patrick's Day   I. Title
GT4995.P3F35 1997   394.2'683
                                         QBI96-40842

Book Design & Layout by C H A S / The Independent Press
Manufactured in the United States of America

10   9   8   7   6   5   4   3   2   1
First Hard-Cover Edition, November, 1997

ACKNOWLEDGEMENTS

The author expresses his gratitude
to those whose contributions were essential—

My wife, Rita Fallon, for her patience
and support; my parents, Betty and
Jim Fallon, for her prayers and his technical
assistance; my sisters, Chris and Jen, for
their party contributions; my daughters,
Lisa and Michelle, for their generous spirit;
my friends, Kevin Moore and Richard
Buellesbach, for their ideas, advice and
help; my dear spiritual friend, Sister
Ann Francis Gleason; Chris Schumacher,
Irish American Foundation, for his website
and faith; Ray O'Flaherty for consultation;
Sister Michele Anne Murphy and all endorsees,
especially Henry Spalding (83 years young)
for his tome on Irish lore and character,
-*Joys of Irish Humor*, an inspiring resource
and recommended reading. Thank you all.

The author —and the publisher— also
thank the following for permission to
use copyrighted material:

BARTH, EDNA—
Shamrocks, Harps, and Shillelaghs
[HOUGHTON-MIFFLIN / CLARION BOOKS,
New York, 1977]

FISHER, AILEEN—
Holiday Programs for Boys and Girls
[PLAYS, INC., Boston MA, 1953 / 1970]

SPALDING, HENRY D.—
Joys of Irish Humor
[JONATHON DAVID PUBLISHERS INC.,
Middle Village NY, 1978 / 1989]

Many of the vintage illustrations used in this volume,
unless otherwise noted (a list of illustrations may be
found on page xviii), have been ascertained to be public
domain.

Regarding written content, every effort has been made
to locate those persons having legal rights or interests
in the material published. We would be grateful to hear
from any copyright holders not here acknowledged.

🕯   🕯   🕯

C O N T E N T S

Carlisle Bridge, Dublin, Ireland. Date unknown.

A LIST OF THE ILLUSTRATIONS

"The Cobbler", by John R. Neill. Circa 1930.

P R E F A C E

by
Sister Michele Anne "Mike" Murphy, PBVM
Principal, Saint John Vianney School

Annually, three shoe boxes make their way from my cellar to my kitchen table. A banner describing them all might read, HEREIN LIE THE MEMORIES AND REMAINS (hats of all sizes, signs, treasured greetings, 'little books,' a green vest, shamrock molds, and, oh yes, a pair of leprechaun shoes—size 8 1/2) OF PAST ST. PATRICK'S DAY GATHERINGS WHICH WILL PROVIDE THE BACKDROP FOR THIS YEAR'S EVENT ON MARCH 17ᵀᴴ. However, the celebration of St. Patrick's Day begins in the Heart —where a spirit of warmth and mirth reaches out to all who gather.

One such gathering I remember was when a certain "O'Fallon" accepted the invitation I gave to a faculty assemblage. His Irish glint enlivened the party to which he brought song, limerick, beverage, and even an Irish play.

*When Irish eyes are smiling, you'd better
watch out. They surelymaybeuptosomething!*

Well, of course, Michael Fallon doesn't
pretend to be the final word on St. Patrick's
Day celebrations! Nonetheless, *The Definitive
St. Patrick's Day Festivity Book* affords all of
us, Irish or not so, the opportunity to have
some informed fun. To be sure, he manages to
deliver some "funny" information in a highly
useful way. Saint Patrick must be honored to
have the record set straight of his missionary
whereabouts and whatabouts, and "Kathleen"
must be relieved to be welcomed home again.
Michael, who obviously has kissed the
Blarney Stone, has been given the power of
sweet, persuasive, clever, and convincing
eloquence as he aptly describes the time,
place, and methods of St. Patrick's Day.
This reader was left with a feeling of having
revisited good times past, and yet learning
ways to enrich next year's event.

I look forward to adding this delightful and useful book to one of my three treasured boxes. On second thought, I may add it to my bookshelf so —with the book in full view— I might remember to open its pages even in June, July, or August. Just as a good friend, this book will remind me to start preparing for the Great Day. I also intend to give this lucky tome to many a friend and relative, for to be sure, it will enhance our celebrations for years to come.

I expect that Michael Fallon's engaging book will quickly make a secure place for itself in the affections of a large body of readers. No doubt, you will want to be one of them....

Happy Saint Patrick's Day
reading and preparing!

—Sister Michele Anne
"Mike" Murphy, PBVM
San Jose, California
Spring, 1996

F O R E W O R D

by the author

WHAT FILLS THE EYE FILLS THE HEART

In 1976, I truly celebrated Saint Patrick's Day for the first time. After years of wearin' the green, drinking green beer, and applauding plain Irish dinners, I was inspired to observe this day in a special way. My motives were to honor my father and our Irish heritage (with due respect to my Polish-German mother).

Together with my sisters we planned a "surprise St. Patrick's Day party," inviting relatives and friends to this weekday affair. Begorrah, if this celebration wasn't a holy success, sure to do the Saint himself proud!

Since that day I have added to the repertory of festivities, and annually celebrate March 17 with great merriment. Sharing this fanfare with friends, in schools, in office gatherings, and at public houses has enlivened St. Patrick's Day for many. I hope the ideas in the pages ahead will bring the same fun rewards for your family and friends—

Erin Go Bragh!

Ireland Forever!

Shrine for the Bell of St. Patrick. Date unknown.

INTRODUCTION

by
Michael James Fallon

WHAT'S GOOD FOR THE GOOSE IS GOOD FOR THE GANDER

Every March 17, people of all nationalities celebrate the feast day of Saint Patrick of Ireland. For those of Irish descent, this occasion is more than a commemoration of St. Patrick's feast day —a few persons actually attend Church services!— it is a day to celebrate our Irish heritage, and in celebrating our heritage, we celebrate ourselves. Numerous others partake in the festivities — for *everyone* is an honorary Irishman on St. Patrick's Day— or they stand by; observing such frivolity with amusement. Why most people respond so enthusiastically to this Irish holiday is left for other analysis, although it has been suggested this holiday may be diversion to winter depression, dispensation of Lenten resolutions, or rationale for imbibition (God forbid!). Perhaps it is the first stirring of the primal instincts of spring that are aroused, for as the Gaelic saying goes—

> *"As the sturgeon or salmon swim exactly in midstream,*
>
> *So does St. Patrick's Day fall exactly in midspring."*

The fact remains that many welcome this opportunity to celebrate culture and to celebrate with others, for everyone is family on St. Patrick's day! To the spirit of "celebration of culture & friendship," this book is dedicated. It provides a variety of ideas for celebrating Saint Patrick's Day. And, while it may seem incredulous that a "How-to-Party" book could be devoted to such a single event; it is intended that the ideas, information, and activities herein may provide useful knowledge, delightful reading, and ideas for other occasions as well. Enjoy!

In contrast to our Irish-American jubilation, the patron saint's feast day is commemorated in Ireland as a national religious holiday. Businesses and schools close, yea, even *pubs* close their doors or limit service to Sunday hours. Family and friends observe this occasion —reverently attending religious services, gathering in homes to enjoy each other's company, celebrating with propriety in music, song and dance; and sharing a meal that includes bacon or mouton, *not* corned beef. Then there is "drowning the shamrock," an old custom to drop the shamrock worn that day into the final glass of whiskey, to toast, to drink, and to throw the shamrock over the left shoulder for luck. However, it is common for the family to pray a blessing—

MAY WE ALL BE ALIVE AND WELL
AND TOGETHER THIS TIME NEXT YEAR

—and then, as Patrick ordained, to take a pot o' whiskey *(pota Phadraig)* and toast his memory. . . .

In all, March 17 is a day of great respect for the man who brought Christianity and compassion to the isle; a missionary effort that recalls their own struggles for survival, for independence, for peace, for national pride and unity.

—M.J.F

Santa Clara, California

17 March 1996

The Definitive
St. Patrick`s Day
Festivity Book

Chapter One

AMBIANCE

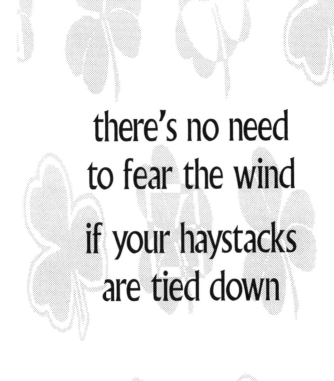

there's no need
to fear the wind
if your haystacks
are tied down

The first step in creating a proper St. Patrick's Day celebration is to create the proper ambiance. Sounds, sights, and appropriate dress can all add to the richness of the day.

Creating A
Visual Environment
of Irish Mystique

⊛ Display Irish culture through pictures, calendars, travel brochures, magazines, books, flags, or a Coat of Arms.

⊛ Put on display St. Patrick's Day greeting cards, and any vacation photos of Ireland!

⊛ Hand drawn artwork fits nicely too—put the kids or early arrivals to work!

⊛ For an action backdrop, have a muted videotape playing. *Darby O'Gill and the Little People* (1959) with actor Sean Connery will surprise and please your guests; and who would not relish glimpses of John Wayne and Maureen O'Hara in *The Quiet Man* (1952).

⊛ Slides of that "once in a lifetime trip

to Eire," illuminated on a back wall, make colorful conversation pieces (assure your guests that you'll not narrate unless called for!).

◉   Post over your porch the Irish Tourist Board standard: a green shamrock with the letters "B&B" underneath. (who knows if boarders might not show up!) Also, hang a welcome sign on your door, in Gaelic: "CEAD MILLE FAILTE" (A Hundred Thousand Welcomes).

◉   Affix the evening's agenda, "IRISH SHENANIGANS," near the social center so all know there are party games planned.

◉   Leave a glass of milk on a window sill marked "FOR THE FAIRY PEOPLE." Ask the aide of someone to surreptitiously sip the milk as if it were indeed drunk by the little folk (though who knows if the offering might not have already disappeared because of actual fairies about!).

Setting the Audio Mood for an Irish Ceili

⊛   Visit music shops and even second hand shops and collect Irish music. Place your music on the stereo at soft volume throughout the celebration. For the Irish Jig and other activities, arrange a portable cassette player and a pre-set tape of Irish / jig tunes.

Now ye are truly blessed if you have friends who are musicians of Irish music and willing to perform. Most Irish dancers and musicians are booked *months* in advance of March 17, so don't expect a miracle. You are twice-blessed if you have a niece or nephew just beginning Irish dance. There's a chance of enlisting their performance for the right amount of bribery. . . .

Costumes to Color
the Consciousness

Donning a costume allows us psychologically to step outside our normal self and become open to new expressions. Encourage your friends to dress-up. At least they should wear something green!

If your friends are unusually bold, suggest costumes of Irish characters, mythical, historical, or stereotypical: SAINT PATRICK (contact your local bishop), LEPRECHAUN (catch one and swap clothes), KING (know any Shakespearean actors?), PRIEST *or* NUN (they'll be wearin' green), DAIRY FARMER (it's the Wellingtons that make the man), JAMES JOYCE or LEOPOLD BLOOM (name tag to self-identify). Not recommended are uniforms of the Irish Republican Army!

For a little embellishment, provide Irish hats. You will be in good company. Sister Michele Anne Murphy, parochial school principal, requires that all faculty wear an Irish hat on the Saint's feast day, and she personally delivers a hat to any teacher who "conveniently forgot" to wear one. As "king or queen of the castle," you have the authority to command the same!

POT O' GOLD, by La Diéh Fawn Geist. 1996

Chapter Two
COMESTIBLES

what butter
and
whiskey will
not cure. . .
there's no cure for

Before an Irish supper of corned beef & cabbage, consider these appetizers. Highlight each food entree with placards. For office party sign-up sheets when a potluck is planned, clever categories incite anticipation.... sure'n we're not speaking blarney! The following ideas will get you started—

The Flag of Ireland: broccoli, cauliflower and carrots diced and arranged in a vertical pattern: Green — White — Orange. Serve with "Shamrock Dip from Shannon."

Irish Potatoes: serve them "chipped" (as in potato chips), "baked", "saladed" (as in potato salad), or "mashed" (as in colcannon). For anyone unfamiliar with Irish cuisine, colcannon is an Irish dish of boiled potatoes and cabbage or kale mashed together and seasoned with minced onion and melted butter. In Irish homes on festive occasions, tokens of fortune may be hid within: a plain gold ring to foretell marriage; a thimble to forebode spinster or bachelorhood; a sixpence coin to prophesy wealth, or a tiny horseshoe to bestow good- luck.

"IRISH BROWNIES" were a brand of chocolate-covered potato chips manufactured by the W. Watson Co., circa 1928.

Cold Celtic Cabbage, *alias* Cole Slaw or Kale Slaw: aye, you wouldn't be callin' this an appetizer now; more an accompaniment to the informal buffet option of corned beef sandwiches and potato salad.

Public House ("Pub") Sandwiches: bar sandwiches —preferably corned beef or ham with cheese— cut in triangular quarters. For a real bar look, spear the sandwiches with olive-topped toothpicks and serve in plastic baskets with chips.

Pub Snacks: (Okay, these are not peculiar to the Irish, just to bar patrons in general.) Naturally include Irish dairy products, yes, we're saying "cheese!" (Sure don't ye' know your friends will be smilin' at this picture too!) If sticking to traditional fare, pass the nuts and pretzels in favor of scones or soda bread. Soda bread is as Irish as the Blarney Stone, so celebrate by treating family and friends to a loaf.

Extravaganza: (for those hosts with barony in their blood) smoked or pickled salmon, salted mackerel, and / or other delights of the Irish sea! After years of corned beef & cabbage, one can imagine an Irish seafood as the delight of vegetarian friends!

Beverages of Ireland: (What would any St. Patrick Day party be without these Irish spirits?)

⊛ GUINNESS STOUT for the stout-hearted man or woman. (I personally recommend Guinness Pub Draught in *cans;* it's creamier and smoother than bottled Guinness, and has a frothy head when poured into a pint glass. . . .)

Other Irish stouts are MURPHY'S and BEAMISH, which are preferred in County Cork and among her sons and daughters.

⊛   HARP ALE for the light angelic drinker. O'DOUL'S for designated drivers, teetotalers, or those competitive souls who wish to stay sharp for the games ahead....

⊛   Wine or Mead. (Mead is an alcoholic drink made from fermented honey and water, popular in Anglo-Saxon days. Irish Castle Banquets start their guests off with mead, to bring a quick warm glow to the evening!)

⊛   Irish Whiskey. Choose your favorite brand, each unique in flavor— BUSHMILLS, JAMESONS, KILBEGGAN, TYRCONNELL, PADDY'S, POWERS, or TULLAMORE DEW. There is also HENNESSY COGNAC and IRISH MIST, again for those of the barony. Sure wouldn't you know that the word "whiskey" comes from the Gaelic *uisce beatha,* which means "water of life!"

⊛   While it's not the common cordial of

Eire itself, feel free to set out Irish Cream Liqueurs like BAILEYS, the true original; CAROLANS, or SAINT BRENDAN'S to name a few. All the cream liqueurs are best either chilled or on the rocks.

❀ For a sweeter or younger crowd, consider a Paddy's Punch— "in-green-ients" can be your secret charm!

"SLAINTE!"

A toast to good luck and good health. Whatever your beverage, be sure and raise a glass in toast to Saint Patrick, to the Irish, and to yourselves. "To Your Health", in Gaelic, is said— *"SLAINTE!"* (pronounced slaun'cha) If you're real good with Gaelic say— *"SLAINTE 'GUS SAOL AGAT,"* (Health and Long Life to You!) Or, if you find yourself slurring its syllables, try another— *"ERIN GO BRAGH!"* (Ireland Forever!)

Irish folklore holds that *"unless the glass you lift contains gentle Irish whiskey, your toast won't work."* Obviously this saying did not hold water with Arthur Guinness' clan. But who believes such folklore anyway?

⊛   And for a purifying lift, be sure to serve, in a clear glass carafe or pitcher, "HOLY WATER FROM KNOCK." (Knock is a place of recent pilgrimage. It's common fact that a devout Churchkeeper saw an apparition of Saint John Apostle with the Blessed Virgin and Child, and all she ever drank, after swearing off the bottle, was local Knock water!)

The Main Course, of course, Corned Beef & Cabbage:
Deciding whether to prepare a main meal to serve later, given that you are master of ceremonies for the evening's activities? Guests may be perfectly content with corned beef sandwiches, potato salad, and cole slaw —a "neo-Irish dinner". On the other hand, you may choose to serve this meal at the end of the evening —a late hour for dinner, but a relaxing conclusion to the festivities.

(Readers undoubtedly have a recipe for cooking corned beef & cabbage, so these notes are intended for bachelors who want to raise this Irish dish to haute cuisine.)

Corned beef varies in quality, and for an Irish pound more (we're not talkin' weight), invest in a choice piece. Soak the meat three hours before cooking. Then, in fresh cold water, simmer the corned beef with pickling spices and / or pepper, one teaspoon dry mustard powder, a sprig of thyme and a sprig of parsley, for several hours according to weight. An onion stuck with cloves can be added one hour before the meat is done, followed by carrots. Halved (red) potatoes can be added the last 40 minutes, and a quartered head of cabbage the last twenty minutes.

Irish Sweets and Treats: ("Saved the best for last?") The dessert menu—

⊛   *Shamrock sugar cookies.*

⊛   *A frosted green shamrock-shaped sheet cake.*

⊛   *Pistachio pudding, mint ice cream,* or *lime sherbet* (excess from your verdant punch concoction!) —all are great finishers to the perfect meal.

⊛   And last but not least —and you thought this elixir was missing from Irish Beverages— the famous Irish Coffee, reportedly first created by one Joe Sheridan, a chef of Shannon, who kindly added a wee bit of the "Irish" to a cup of coffee for cold and war-weary Yanks returning home after World War II. The world-famous Buena Vista Café in San Francisco is now known as the "Home of the Irish Coffee in America." This is where newspaper columnist Stanton Delaplane first brought the recipe from the Shannon Airport. The directions they give for this quintessential elixir are as follows—

IRISH COFFEE

—Fill Irish whiskey glasses or durable wine glasses with warm water and let sit.

—Empty glasses and drop 3 cubes or spoonfuls of sugar into each.

—Cover with enough coffee to stir and dissolve sugar.

—Add a jigger of Irish whiskey to each.

—Then fill with coffee to within one-quarter inch of rim.

—Top with real dairy whipped cream.

Admire, then raise the glass and....
"Ah, Slainte."

PLEASE NOTE: The Irish, despite their prover-
bial proclivity for the drink, have more than
a couple proverbs of caution, but here are
two of the best—

IT IS SWEET TO DRINK BUT BITTER TO PAY FOR.

and,

*THIRST IS THE END OF DRINKING
AND SORROW IS THE END OF DRUNKENNESS.*

After a celebration of culture and friendship,
nothing could be more heart-rending than
consequences of over-indulgence. Exercise
good judgment in limiting or pre-empting
liquor consumption at the proper time. Post
or express your concern and intentions at the
outset. A sobering note, yes, but it must be
said!

Chapter Three
INTONATION

time is a
great storyteller

Now that guests have gathered and friends have acquainted themselves (all the while reacting to your outlandish efforts to set an ambiance) and have become accustomed to the ridiculous Irish hats you insisted top their heads (yet having satisfied their stomachs and warmed their hearts to Gaelic-hour hors d'oeuvres), you are ready to call the celebration to formal commencement. (No, this call to arms does not require singing the Irish National Anthem, though everyone is welcome to such patriotism, for sure!) It is politically correct, however, that anyone truly celebrating this day would acknowledge the saint for whom this day of honor is declared.

You (or your designee) will recall those dreaded days of yesteryear when, as "parochial" school student, after choosing the saint of your choice, and having completed your research (euphemism for homework), you mustered the courage to stand in front of your classmates and tell the story of your saint, while your all-knowing teacher, Sister All-Saints'-Name, looked on with sweet admiration.

St. Patrick, Patron Saint of Ireland.
Detail of unfinished pencil portrait.

The stage is set, and begorrah, we've done the homework for you! And once you succeed in calling your friends to order, getting their attention (not necessarily their respect), the high Saint of Ireland can be saluted and his praises read straight from this prepared text. Abbreviate the Story of Patrick as you will given the interest level —yours or theirs.

The Story of Saint Patrick, Patron Saint of Ireland

Around the year 400A.D., Patrick was born in Scotland. When he was yet a boy, the Ard-Ri, —High King of Ireland, Niall of the Nine Hostages by name— swept across the sea and captured his village. Patrick was taken to Ireland, sold as a slave, and sent to herd sheep and swine. There in northeast Ireland, in his solitude and suffering, Patrick discovered the one true God, and, to this Creator God he pledged his life. Years later and now a young man, Patrick dreamed a vision, and following that vision, he escaped and struggled home to his family. After years of religious study to become a priest and missionary, Patrick dreamed of returning to Ireland; often hearing in his dreams the voice of the Irish— *"crying to thee, come hither and walk with us once more."* Eventually Pope Celestine fulfilled Patrick's wish and commissioned him as bishop to preach the gospel to the Celtic people. Patrick came as the rising sun to the eastern shore of Ireland, and commenced an incredible mission across Ireland, preaching and baptizing, ordaining priests and bishops, erecting churches, and establishing places of learning and worship.

Such heroic feats in primitive time were not without difficulty and danger. Yea, such is the making of legends.

One legend tells of Patrick lighting the Easter bonfire on the hill of Slane on the night when it was forbidden to kindle any other fire in Ireland before the high King's own fire blazed from the royal ramparts of Tara. Seeing Patrick's paschal torch, the King sent a war-band to kill the saint and douse the blaze. But, the fire could not be quenched; and Patrick, with his companions, passed through the warriors in the guise of a herd of deer. They came safely to Tara, where Patrick defeated the royal druids in a contest of miracle-working. Many in the King's court bowed down and were converted, and though the King himself was not one of them, he did honor Patrick with the right to preach freely.

Another legendary account is told of Patrick and his companions arriving at sunrise at the royal center of ancient paganism where they discovered the two daughters of the King, Eithne the Red and Fedelm the Fair. These two closely questioned Patrick about God, to which he recited the Holy Creed. Desiring to see the Christ, they asked to be baptized. Upon receiving the sacrament, the girls died on the spot and were buried there.

One final tale has Patrick coming to a Neolithic tomb thought to be a "giant's grave." To satisfy his companions' curiosity, Patrick raised from the dead the pagan giant, baptized him, and returned him to his grave.

In time, Patrick and his missionaries converted

the island to Christianity. Praying and fasting atop what is now Croagh Patrick, the Saint extracted from God Himself the promise that the Irish would hold fast to the faith until the end of time, and that on the day of doom—

> *"I, Patrick, shall be*
> *judge of the men of Erin."*

———————————

Upon his death, in 465A.D., several communities contended for the honor of his burial. Tradition has it that the body of Patrick, wrapped in its shroud, was placed upon a cart drawn by two white oxen. The beasts were unreined and wandered to Downpatrick where, it is said, now lies the remains of the Saint, his gravestone a granite boulder marked with a cross and simply inscribed: **PATRIC**. Supposedly at his passing, the sun would not set, but shone in the sky for *twelve* days and nights, refusing to make a new day without him. Today, a stained-glass window in Saint Patrick's Cathedral Dublin reflects the Saint's own summary confession—

*I am greatly a debtor to God
who hath vouchsafed me such great grace
that many people by my means
should be born again to God.*

A.D.387—ST. PATRICK
APOSTLE OF IRELAND—465A.D.

Beyond His Own Great Accomplishments,
Several Legends Evolved Around His Feats.
These Delightful Legends of Patrick Regard:

The Serpents. The most famous legend about St. Patrick is that he miraculously drove snakes and all venomous beasts from the island by banging a drum, and did this so well that to touch Irish soil is instant death for any such creature. Even Irish wood has a virtue against poison, so that it is reported of King's College, Cambridge, that *"being built of Irish wood, no spider doth ever come near it."*

The Shamrock. Patrick, sent to preach the gospel to heathens, found that the pagan Irish had great difficulty comprehending the doctrine of the Trinity until he gave them a natural example by holding up a shamrock to show the three leaves combined to make a single plant. The Irish understood at once, and the shamrock became the symbol of the land. Irishmen wear it in their hats on the saint's day.

His Death. When Patrick was dying on this day, circa 465A.D., he urged his friends not to lament, but rather to celebrate his exit into everlasting life. To this end, his last request was that each of them take a wee drop of something to drink to ease their pain. Out of reverence for the Saint, and in compliance with his last words, is supposed to have come the Irish predilection for whiskey.

March 17. It is the death of Saint Patrick on this day, and his universal recognition as the patron saint of Ireland, that led to the celebration of March 17 as Saint Patrick's Day. Its emphasis in Ireland is a holy religious time with appropriate praying, singing and dance. The first North American celebration was held in Boston in 1737 by the Irish Charitable Society, and later in Philadelphia and New York City by the Friendly Sons of St. Patrick and the Ancient Order of Hibernians.In the archives of the Ancient Order of Hibernians, rests a book by John D. Crimmins, 1902, entitled— *ST. PATRICK'S DAY: ITS CELEBRATION IN NEW YORK AND OTHER AMERICAN PLACES, 1737-1845. HOW THE ANNIVERSARY WAS OBSERVED BY REPRESENTATIVE IRISH ORGANIZATIONS, AND THE TOASTS PROPOSED.* Another source states that on March 17, 1762, a group of Irish-born soldiers, en route to the local tavern of renown to honor their patron saint, staged the first parade in colonial New York, complete with marching bands and colorful banners. Bystanders and passersby joined the promenade, singing Irish ballads and dancing down the cobblestones. The event was so joyful, it was repeated yearly.

Commentary on Saint Patrick

Saint Patrick's mission was most successful: Ireland was almost entirely Christian by the time of his death. He understood and wisely preserved the country's social structure, converting the people tribe by tribe. He introduced the Roman alphabet, and at his insistence, the traditional laws of Ireland were codified and the harsher ones mitigated, particularly those that dealt with slavery and taxation of the poor. In 457A.D. he retired to Saul, where four years later, he died. He was buried in Downpatrick, which was a great European shrine until its destruction by the English government in 1539.

Saint Patrick is remembered by the Irish as the architect of the Catholic Church in Ireland, and also for his engaging personality. He was a man of warmth and deep understanding of the people's strengths as well as their frailties. He could, and would, share a drink with them, and convert them the next day. He possessed a lively sense of humor and enjoyed a good joke as well as any of his followers. Small wonder then that a body of humorous literature has been created about him, for he is recalled with earthy affection as well as reverence. This earthy affection and reverence is reflected in an Irish Ballad of familial attachment to the Saint which appears in *Joys of Irish Humor,* by Henry D. Spalding. . . .

Saint Patrick Was A Gentleman

St. Patrick was a gentleman
He came of decent people.
In Dublin town he built a church,
And on it put a steeple.

His father was a Callahan,
His mother was a Brady,
His aunt was an O'Shaughnessy,
And his uncle was a Grady.

Conversely, another poem attests to *his* affinity and affection to the people and their drink—

"St. Patrick of Ireland, My Dear!"

A fig for St. Denis of France—
He's a trumpery fellow to brag on;
A fig for St. George and his lance,
Which spitted a heathenish dragon;
And the saints of the Welshman or Scot
Are a couple of pitiful pipers;
Both of whom may just travel to pot,

Compared with that patron of swipers,[1]
St. Patrick of Ireland, my dear!
He came to the Emerald Isle
On a lump of a paving stone mounted;
The steamboat he beat by a mile,
Which mighty good sailing was counted.
Says he, "The salt water I think
Has made me most fishily thirsty;
So bring me a flagon of drink
To keep down the mulligrubs,[2] burst ye—
Of drink that is fit for a saint."
The flagon he lifted in sport
(Believe me, I tell you no fable),
A gallon he drank from the quart,
And then placed it full on the table.
"A miracle!" everyone said,
And they all took a haul at the stingo;
They were capital hands at the trade,
And drank till they fell; yet, by jingo,
The pot still frothed over the brim.
You've heard, I suppose, long ago,
How the snakes, in a manner most antic,

1 —*A drinker of malt liquor*
2 —*Colic, ill-temper*

He marched to the County Mayo,
And trundled them into th' Atlantic.
Hence, not to use water for drink,
The people of Ireland determine;
With mighty good reason, I think,
Since St. Patrick has filled it with vermin,
And vipers and other such stuff.
Oh, he was an elegant blade
As you'd meet from Fairhead to Kilcrumper;
And though under the sod he is laid,
Yet here goes his health in a bumper!
I wish he was here, that my glass
He might by art magic replenish!
But since he is not — why alas!
My ditty must come to a finish,
Because all the liquor is out.

—William Maginn

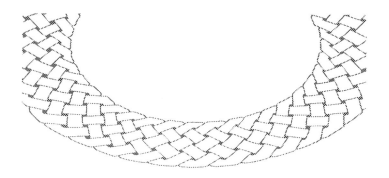

Now that the official history of Saint Patrick has been duly and properly established; and as such pronouncements quickly are subject to humor, it is recommended that YOU yourself "showtime" the way into entertaining your audience. With a little forethought but a lot of stimulus (book of Irish comedy, shot of Irish whiskey), you can improvise a comic routine. However, knowing that is precisely why you bought this book, sure 'n we're providin' some ideas. Just one requisite remains solely your doing, to surrender to that irrepressible urge to talk in brogue. You'll be thought none-the-less for it, even if you end up soundin' like you come from God-knows-where. Often it's the attempted brogue itself that holds your friends incredulous!

St. Patrick's Day Humor Sampler
by Michael J. Fallon

Ah, what a fine day is Saint Paddy's Day!
From the moment I arise
til I lay me' head upon the pillow at night,
It's a day of mirth and laughter.
But I tell ye now,
Ye's got to be aware that on this day
the LEPRECHAUNS ARE MOST
      UP TO THEIR TRICKS,
almost in a kind of satirical honor
to the great Saint himself
who wouldn't always be approvin'
      of their ways,
that is, if the Saint ever allowed
      even a thought that
the fairy folk were for real,
given that his Catholic faith
didn't allow for belief in superstitions an' all.
But I tell ye, leprechauns are for real,
Irish legends of the Wee Folk are lengthy,

and I'd be believin' myself, ye know,
as they've played their shenanigans on me!
(and no, I wasn't tippin' no bottle
        at the time, either!)
Well, when I climbed out of bed this mornin'
and made my way to th' bathroom,
lo and beholdin' if I didn't find there
a POT O' GOLD!
But then I be sayin' to myself
"It might just be what I left behind
after an evenin' at the pub."
Then I stepped into the shower and
        what do I find?
me usual bar of soap?
Heavens no, it's become a
        BAR of IRISH SPRING!
It's then that I be rememberin' what day it is.
I greet me wife and say to her "BLESS YOU"
and she says to me: "I didn't sneeze."
So I be remindin' her that it's St. Patrick's Day
and that she ought to be a wearin' green,
and also the button I give 'er that says
"KISS ME, I'M IRISH".

but she replies back to me,
"You're Irish, I'm not, and don't be usin'
that blarney on me, Michael O'Fallon".
I tell her not to worry about wearin' the button
"KISS ME, I'M IRISH",
the old maid down the road's been
wearin' that button for three weeks now
and it doesn't seem t' do any good.
Well, I make my way down t' breakfast
and ask me wife how she wants her coffee.
She says to me: "IRISH"
and sure'n I'm glad to hear
she's gettin' the spirit.
Now every mornin' I pour myself
a bowl of granola cereal.
Well what do you think comes out
of the bloomin' box this day?
LUCKY CHARMS!
I tell ye, those leprechauns are rascals.
I put clover honey on my cereal
and what do you think springs up?
SHAMROCKS, of course.
I let out an expletive and my wife shouts:

"What's happening down there?"
I say "NUTTIN, HONEY"
—she just wouldn't believe it either.
On the way out the door I inform her
          that I'll be home late,
as I'm meetin' with four Irish
          friends after work.
She responds: Sure'n WHEREVER YOU
          FIND FOUR IRISHMEN,
YOU'LL ALWAYS FIND A FIFTH!
So now I'm about to head off to work
and me darn car won't start.
I check it out and what do I find but
A POTATO IN THE EXHAUST PIPE!
Now who'd ye think played a trick
          like that, tell me?
So finally I'm drivin' to work
an' I look around at what a grand day it is:
the GRASS IS GREEN,
the LIGHTS TURN GREEN,
PEOPLE BE DRESSED IN GREEN,
An' my only wish is to be
          ROLLIN' IN THE GREEN

—THAT'S THE GREEN HILLS
    OF IRELAND.
Ah, March 17, tis a great day,
    SAINT PATRICK'S DAY,
An' especially if yer Irish.
Enjoy your CORNED BEEF & CABBAGE
(Where's the potato?)
and don't be drinkin' too much
    of the GUINNESS.
Be especially careful of mixin' your drinkin'
with IRISH WHISKEY,
you never know what such mixin'
    could lead to!
Best be savin' that jigger for
    the IRISH COFFEE.
An' once ag'in remember,
Look out for LEPRECHAUNS
    and their SHENANIGANS.
FAITH 'N BEGORRAH to you all,
And let me be endin' my words
with an IRISH BLESSIN'—

"MAY ALL THE JOY
THAT ECHOES THROUGH
A HAPPY IRISH SONG,
AND ALL THE LUCK THE
SHAMROCK BRINGS
BE YOURS THE WHOLE YEAR LONG,
MAY YOU HAVE BLESSINGS,
PLEASURES & FRIENDS
TO GLADDEN ALL LIFE'S WAY,
AND MAY ST. PATRICK SMILE ON YOU
TODAY AND EVERYDAY."

A LETTER FROM MUM BACK HOME IN IRELAND

(Copied from a parchment in an Irish bar
and mailed to the author for St. Patrick's Day.)

Dear Son,

Happy Saint Patrick's Day to you! I trust you be receivin' this letter in time for the holiday. Just a few lines to let you know that we're still alive. I'm writing this s-l-o-w-l-y because I know that you can't read fast. Also, you won't know the house when you get home, as we have moved.

About your father, he's got a lovely new job. He has five hundred men under him. He cuts grass in the cemetery.

Your brother, Barry, picked up a newly arrived American in his taxi two weeks ago, and wished him a pleasant stay in Ireland. When he picked him up for his return flight home and asked him if he enjoyed his stay, the American said, "No, it was too cold, too wet, and he didn't like the Irish." Well, your brother dropped his bags right then and there and told him "Next vacation you can go to hell. It'll be hot enough, it'll be dry, and there won't be any Irishmen!" Your brother does have a temper, but a wit too, I might add.

Your sister, Mary, had a baby this morning. I haven't found out yet whether it's a boy or a girl, so I don't know if you are an uncle or an aunt.

I went to the doctor's on Thursday and your father came with me. The doctor put a small tube in my mouth and told me not to talk for ten minutes. Your father offered to buy it from him.

Your grand uncle Patrick drowned last week in a vat of Irish Whiskey at the Dublin Brewery. God rest his soul. Some of his workmates tried to save him but he fought them off bravely. They cremated him and it took three days to put out the fire.

It only rained twice this week, first for three days and then for four days. It's depressing. We had a letter come from the undertaker. He said if the last payment on your grandmother's plot wasn't paid in seven days —up she comes!

Well, that's all the news. Like I say, don't be forgettin' your parents now, back here in Eire; you livin' it up in America an' all. Remember to write some time.

Your Loving Mother

P.S.— I was goin' to send you a five pound note, but I already sealed the envelope. Be good son. And don't you go drinkin' too much on Saint Paddy's.

(And while me mum was thoughtful enough to send a letter, me father generously sent along some clippings —of local news, that is. You didn't think I meant "grass clippings" from his job, did ya?)

Top o' the Mornin' Times

REPORTIN' THE BLARNEY FROM OL' KILLARNEY

ST. PADDY'S DAY PARADE PARTICIPANTS IN CONTROVERSY

Seems everyone knows what's best for the St. Patrick's Day Parade, but no one knows what's best for all the participants. The Faith n' Begorrah Christian Group objects to the Liberated Ladies of Hibernia's entry, "Erin Go Bra-less." The Ladies in turn resent the Gaelic Fellows carrying their shillelaghs in hand, fearing someone will get poked. The Friendly Sons of Saint Patrick, in spirit of compromise, offered to parade in paddy wagons to keep the peace. Tinkering with tradition, the Tinkers' Caravan was aligned second to last because of the high pitch of their tinwhistles, while MacNamara's Band objects to marching behind the Tinkers' with their large number of horses, ponies, and dogs. The city mayor commented, "Saint Patrick help us!"

MOTHER MACHREE'S VISITED BY MEAL MARAUDER

At Mother Machree's Boarding House for wayward women, a mid-day marauder dropped a pair of woolen trousers into the pot of chowder Mrs. Murphy left cooking on the stove. Mrs. Murphy hated to point a finger, but several names surfaced along with the bubbling pant leg. Among them were: The Irish washerwoman, upset over lost wages for unaccounted stout stains on white blouses; Molly Malone whose cockles and mussels were passed over in favor of Molly Flander's flounder in the selection of ingredients; and Mrs. O'Leary who has been acting strangely ever since her cow was deported to Chicago and gained notoriety never achieved in the County Kerry Fair.

MUCKROSS HOUSE HUSBANDRY AWARD TO 'BABE' THE PIG

Following her academy award nomination as the sheep herding pig of Skibbereen, 'Babe' squealed away with the Oscar Wilde Award at the Muckross House Husbandary Pageant. The award was given for earnest achievement in a human endeavor. Babe was honored for her Alternative Fat Free Vegetarian Irish Cookbook. Commenting on

File Photo by La Diéh Fawn Geist

(continued next page)

her citation, Babe oinked, "This recognition is no spam, it speaks for the lifeblood of all Irish livestock." Also receiving an Oscar was Paddy McGinty's goat, for her rise from undocumented nanny to a successful billy goat labor organizer. This year's lifetime achievement award was bestowed posthumously upon Ray O'Flaherty's drake, Mallard, for his early roles in *Darby O'Gill and the Little People* (1959), *The Quiet Man* (1952), and more recently as back-up singer in *The Commitments* (1991), and IRA undercover agent in *The Crying Game* (1992).

S P O R T S
NOTRE DAME AND NAVY DUKE IT OUT IN DUBLIN

The "Fighting Irish" and Midshipmen meet this fall on Irish turf in their own version of Irish football. The nickname, "Fightin' Irish," goes back to when we honored warriors in our culture. The expression came to America with the large number of Irish soldiers who fought alongside George Washington against the Brits. ND adopted the name for their sports teams, and the Virgin atop the golden dome winced, for athletes carry the reputation on and off the field! Give 'em a good fightin' match, Midshipmen, but if you're goin' down, remember the "Unsinkable Molly Brown" survived the Titanic, attributing her good fortune to "Irish luck." So, the "luck of the Irish" be with you both, boys, especially after the contest!

LEPRECHAUN SUES BAR PATRON FOR PERSONAL LIABILITY

In an unprecedented class action suit, a Leprechaun named Liam is bringing litigation against Casey Muldoon for reckless behavior endangering the lives of leprechauns. It seems Casey stumbled out of the local pub one night last week after drowning the shamrock in anticipation of Saint Patrick's Day, and, wheeling his shillelagh like a sickle to clear a path in front of him, he laid low the leprechaun. Next mornin', Casey swore 'twas but a dream, until a court summons was delivered to his door. Casey stammered, "I'll look forward to seeing that little fellow in court!" Likely he won't, however, Liam is being represented by Sir Hillary Hemlock, lawyer for the Druid Society, and is seeking an undisclosed amount of gold bullion.

(Finally, here is a little extra
humor on the stereotyping of the Irish!)

The Native Irishman
by a Converted Saxon

Before I came across the sea
    to this delightful place,
I thought the native Irish were
    a funny sort of race;

I thought they bore shillelag-sprigs
    and that they always said:
"Och hone, acushla, tare-an-ouns,
    begorrah" and "bedad!"

I thought they sported crownless
    hats with dhudeens in the rim;
I thought they wore long trailing coats
    and knickerbockers trim;
I thought they went about the place as
    tight as they could get,
And that they always had a fight with
    everyone they met.

I thought their noses all turned up just
    like a crooked pin;
I thought their mouths six inches wide
    and always on the grin;
I thought their heads were made of steel,
    as hard as any nails;
I half suspected that they were possessed
    of little tails.

But when I came unto the land
of which I heard so much,
I found that the inhabitants were
not entirely such;
I found their features were not at all
exactly like baboons;
I found that some wore billycocks
and some had pantaloons.

I found their teeth were quite as
small as Europeans' are,
And that their ears, in point of size,
were not peculiar.
I even saw a face or two which might
be handsome called;
And by their very largest feet I was
not much appalled.

I found them sober now and then;
and even in the street
It seems they do not have a fight
with every boy they meet.
I even found some honest men among

the very poor;
And I have heard some sentences
 which did not end with "shure."

It seems that praties[1] in their skins
 are not their only food,
And that they have a house or two
 which is not built of mud.
In fact, they're not all brutes or
 fools, and I suspect that when
They rule themselves they'll be
 as good, almost, as Englishmen!

—Anonymous

1 —*Praties: Irish Potatoes*

Chapter Four
IRISH SWEEPSTAKES

you'll never
plough a field

by turning it over
in your mind

No purchase necessary to win, and most guests delight in testing their knowledge of the Irish and matching wits with one another.

These contests work well when informally set out to pick up and play as guests gather and partake of the buffet. Prizes are the host's prerogative; some guests may be content with the personal challenge or team problem-solving, others may be motivated by *"to the victor belong the spoils."* (Cromwell was one of these, just ask the Irish!)

IRISH WORD SCRAMBLE

Directions: Unscramble these words related to Irish culture. . . .

(For those needing answers, see the Glossary in the Chapter "Blarney," page 203)

NITSA RAPIKTC	KASRMOCH
OTOATP	AHPR
IEGCLA	SILSEBNG
EIPP	BAIRWON
ANURECLEHP	ESIL LADMERE
TOP O' DOGL	RSIHI TEWS

GALHLESLHI   RIDDUS
LEICCT SROSC   EEHSNAB
CLUBIP USHOE   CLADDAGH
SHEIKWY SRIHI   GOB PATE
ERLAYBN NOTES   NSNGEAHISNA
TANIS DRIIGB   FO SLELK OKOB

IRISH CITIES & LANDMARKS
"A Driving Tour of Ireland"

If you've toured Ireland, you'll likely recognize this circle route and these landmarks. Match the sites with their description by connecting lines.

(Answers in "Blarney," page 213)

LIMERICK	has customs for coming or going duty free
BUNRATTY CASTLE	fishermen wives keep tourists in stitches
CLIFFS OF MOHER	"everybody must get stoned" coaxes Bob Dylan
ARAN ISLANDS	medieval diner dishing banquets and culture
GALWAY	St. Finbar's plug for altar wine, oft-popped
CROAGH PATRICK	Atlantic test for leap of faith
KNOCK	"cove" in Gaelic, not "corn-on-the-stalk"
DONEGAL	mountain Patrick croaked of climbing, by God!
RIVER SHANNON	"woolen sweaters on sale" cheep the birds
DUBLIN	seagals flock to see horse races in summer
RIVER LIFFEY	"dark pool" in Gaelic, likely spilt stout
TRINITY COLLEGE	real horses, real men, sow wild oats and foal
IRISH STUD FARM	holy water packs a punch swears churchkeeper
WATERFORD	city of humorous poetry wrote Edward Lear
TIPPERARY	jaunting round Muckross Estate, step rightly
CORK	no hay penny? a half penny will do to cross
BLARNEY CASTLE	loughs flow down by this old mill stream
COBH	like sheep that pass on the right?
RING OF KERRY	Father, Son & Holy Ghost are professors here
LAKES OF KILLARNEY	dairy town tipped the, er —milk bottle daily!
SHANNON	hear the crystal sound of breaking glass

"IRELAND PERSONIFIED." Circa early 1900's

AN IRISH BOXING MATCH:
AUTHORS & LITERATURE

Climb into the ring of Irish literature: Match the Irish author with his literary piece by connecting lines.

(Answers in "Blarney," page 217)

SAINT PATRICK   Believed in *Importance of Being Earnest*

SAMUEL BECKET   *Borstal Boy* busted by the Brits

BRENDAN BEHAN   Gave *Confession* to his mission in Erin

JAMES JOYCE   A real *Playboy of the Western World*

SEAN O'CASEY   His play was a real *Cock-a-Doodle Dandy*

GEORGE BERNARD SHAW   Has nightmares about *Lilliputians*

JONATHAN SWIFT   Portrayed *Ulysses* as a young man

JOHN MILLINGTON SYNGE   Wrote poetry to *Wild Swans at Coole*

OSCAR WILDE   Still *Waiting For Godot*

WILLIAM BUTLER YEATS   His *Pygmalion* created my fair lady

IRISH LIMERICK WRITING CONTEST

The limerick is a form of humorous verse, taking its name from the city of Limerick, Ireland. No one knows how it originated. The limerick is a poem of *five* lines; the first two lines rhyme with the fifth, the third with the fourth. Limericks often poke fun at people, and not all would please good Patrick! The first line often begins— "There was a..." and ends with the name of a person or place; the last line ending with a far-fetched rhyme. Edward Lear's *A Book of Nonsense* (1846) made the form popular. Here are two typical limericks by Lear.

There was a young lady of Wilts,

Who walked up to Scotland on stilts;

When they said it is shocking

To show so much stocking,

She answered, "Then what about kilts?"

There was a young lady whose chin

Resembled the point of a pin;

So she had it made sharp,

And purchased a harp,

And played several tunes with her chin.

Now are you ready to write a loony limerick of your own? Here is a model to help get you started.

There once was a—

Who—

S/He. . . .

And. . . .

And—

Note: Limericks are listed in the Chapter, "Irish Shenanigans," as part of another gaming activity, Limerick Charades. Guests might share their limerick creations at that time. . . .

A PINT O' GUINNESS STOUT

An activity for a drinking crowd, fashionable in this period of microbrewery beer tasting (a newer vintage of the wine-tasting trend), is imported from a St. Patrick's Day, *"Win Your Own Irish Pub"* contest sponsored by Guinness Import Company. There were two versions in three successive years: DESCRIBE YOUR PERFECT PINT OF GUINNESS, and DESCRIBE YOUR MOST MEMORABLE PINT OF GUINNESS. The "wee people" suggest "raising a glass" in gaming format by inviting friends —beer drinkers or not— to sample a swig or more of stout.

In turn, giving each person center stage, while proudly upholding a glass of stout, have him/her wax poetic, and describe either—

I. their taste experience of drinking this "perfect pint" of beer; or,

II. their "most memorable pint" ever (of any such brew).

"Wee people" believe your group will find the

responses quite diverse, quite descriptive, and the memories touching! Excuse this author for taking opportunity to display his own "non-winning" entries, including one in limerick.

A perfect pint o' Guinness stout—
pours slow, smooth; tumbling,
        bubbling brown
foams before dark elixir spirit settles
thrice drawn, topped, til at last
a frothy creamy head so thick
supports your lip marks every sip
stout slowly savored,
        mouth-watering swallowed
—is satisfying as mother's milk.

A perfect pint o' Guinness stout
distills in every village pub where
Arthur Guinness hangs his
        black & orange seal;
where Irish folk gather with
warm smiles on red freckled faces,
quick ta' quiver a quip in brogue

with a leprechaun's twinkle of eye,
raising frothy pints in toast o' "Slainte".

A perfect pint o' Guinness stout

Poured creamy brown, and drinking
leaves no doubt

Irish spirits fill your glass

tasteful memories that last

Good friends, good health,
good mirth sweet Harp plays out.

Darby O'Gill entered the pub, potato sack
slung over his shoulder.
"I have in here *Brian Boru,* King of
Leprechauns" he boasted.
To prove it he handed down a full pint
into the sack,
as quickly the glass was returned —*empty!*

Enchanted, I ordered another pint
    o' Guinness myself!

Awaiting the ceili, we were sippin'
    our pints o' Guinness quietly,
when a matron swore she'd seen me' father
    heretofore, though it weren't true.
Amending, she professed to have a
    daughter "most beautiful".
I replied, "she's taken after her mother."
    She says in turn to me' father,
"your son speaks glib as Guinness."

One damp, gray, cloudy day, in a
    churchyard under Ben Bulben,
my father and I paid our respects at the grave
    of William Butler Yeats.
Then in a pub before a peat fire burning,
    we warmed ourselves with
pints o' Guinness, and *"cast a cold eye*
    on life on death."

Good sportsmanship accepts defeat, and congratulates the victors with respect. And so I salute the Winners' Essays, presented with highest regard, compliments of Guinness Imports....

Guinness is . . . the taste of full-bodied life.
It will not go gently into a bland,
        cautious existence.
Taste the complex layers through
        Irish pub history
woven with the rich warmth of community.
Guinness reminds you that beer is meant
        to be alive,
as you are —distinct, flavorful, and strong.

—Mrs. Shann Weston,
Portland, Oregon

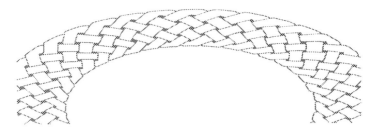

They carried me into the bar.
    "Make way—" shouted one.
"A pint of Guinness," ordered another.
The rich, cool, dark, white-collared
    Guinness was presented.
The first sip awakened my senses;
    the second brought me to the reality—
I Had Done It! At age fifty, I completed
    the Boston Marathon!

Mr. Frank E. Gallagher,
Fort Lauderdale, FL

The process.
The bar.
The stool.

    The bartender.
    The question.
    The answer.

        The usual.
        The Guinness.
        The glass.

The tap.
The pour.
The wait.

    The topping.
    The scrape.
    The serving.

        The pint.
        The bill.
        The pay.

    The tip.
    The sip.
    The pleasure.

The wipe.
The smile.
The taste.

The best.

                Mr. John "Jay" Mulligan,
                South Boston, MA

An added word or two —symptomatic of the gift of gab that likewise flows from the tap— on Guinness, paraphrased from the May1996 issue of *Bon Appétit:*

"In the pubs of Ireland, Guinness stout flows slowly from the tap, filling expectant glasses as if it had been drawn directly from deep within the Irish earth....No other brand in the whole world is tied so closely to a national identity as Guinness is to Ireland...The rich black stout from Guinness accounts for seven of every ten pints consumed in Ireland, and in itself —hearty, assertive, complex— is a fitting symbol of the stalwart Irish character."

And,

"Talking folklore...In the 1800's, Guinness was recommended to nursing mothers. It was also recommended as a bath for newborns and was thought to be an aphrodisiac. In a later era, Guinness was touted by physicians as a cure-all, and its advertising slogan was 'GUINNESS IS GOOD FOR YOU.' In 1936, according to Leslie Dunking, author of *The Guinness Drinking Companion*, when the Federal Alcohol Administration objected to the advertising, Guinness company produced letters from doctors which said that Guinness was indeed good for anemia, insomnia, neuralgia, post-influenza debility, and depression.' Of course, we suspect those doctors were all Irish!

"The slogan, Guinness is Good for You, has remained the basis of Guinness advertising overseas. The line came from a British advertising campaign of the 1920's which asked drinkers why they favored Guinness. The universal response? 'Because it does me good.'"

[Author's note: Unofficial beverage consumption totals have the Irish consuming 10 million pints of stout a day —twice the entire population of the Isle!]

Old Parliament House, Dublin, Ireland. Date unknown.

Chapter Five

SHENANIGANS

any man
can lose his hat
in a fairy wind

Though requiring preparation, the "wee
people" deem these shenanigans the *Best of
Games—*

Potato Fortune Hunt

Sublime potatoes! that, from Antrim's shore

To famous Kerry, form the poor man's store;

Agreeing well with every place and state—

The peasant's noggin, or the rich man's plate.

A brief historical note to be read before the game
begins: During the 1800's, Irish people depended on
potatoes for food. The typical Irish family ate potatoes
three times a day, year in and year out. In good years,
under ideal conditions, a farmer managed to harvest
sixty barrels a year; a barely adequate food supply for a
family. But from 1845-1847, Ireland's potato crop
failed because of a plant disease....

In the Irish Potato Famine of 1845-1850, one million
died of starvation and two million fled the country, most
to the United States. Many of us or our Irish friends are
in the US today as a result.

Before your St. Patrick's Day celebration,
carefully pick spuds from the grocery stand,
looking for specimens that "bat an eye or

two." Post the chart of Potato Fortunes which follows. Hide the spuds about the house (taking note where, lest you discover a decomposing potato later!).

Instructions: Announce to your guests that the "Great Potato Fortune Hunt" is to begin. Set the boundaries, time limit, and number of spuds to be found. You may give, as playful motivation— *"these are the potatoes needed to cook for dinner, lest a 'famine' occur in this house!"* To toss some confusion into the hunt, call out "hot" or "cold" as diggers search....

Conclusion: When time is up, have participants check the number of "eyes" on their collected potato(s) and *read their fortune* according to Irish superstition. Consider pairing-up those "compatible by fortune," e.g., foe—friend; presents—happily married; suitor—courtship, travel—wealth; broken hearts—single blessedness. Have individuals or pairs share their good(?) fortune with the group. Finally, caution guests to check their automobile exhaust pipes before they drive home, as leprechauns are known to be about (evidence

the sipped "fairy milk glass on window sill"),
and have pulled such a prank before!

Potato Fortunes
The number of eyes on your potato
tells your fortune—

1	—Foes	6	—Courtship
2	—Presents	7	—Wealth
3	—Friends	8	—Broken Heart
4	—Suitors	9	—Happily Married
5	—Travel	10	—Single Blessedness

LEPRECHAUN, by La Diéh Fawn Geist. 1996

The Potato Jig

In groups of 5-7 people, with one potato in hand per group, what could be more fitting on this grand day than all should partake in an Irish Jig? But not to worry, you're not askin' them to dance —just yet! Hand out to each group the following jog. Instruct each group to pass around the potato, a kind of hands-on "hot potato" game. When you say the magic word "JIG," the person holding the potato begins the actual jig verse with the word *"RIGGIDY"* while passing the potato to either person right or left of him / her, who says— *"HIGGIDY"* and passes the potato on to *"WIGGIDY,"* and so on until one person goes "OUT." Repeat the game until each group has a winner. All group winners then vie for final champion: "King Paddy."

Now, before "King Paddy" is presented his / her prize, there is one last condition. (Have your Irish jig song and portable cassette player ready.) King Paddy must *"dance an Irish Jig."* Give him / her center stage for all to see, and initiate clapping from the bystanders.

Such a feat ought to be deserving of a great prize: a stuffed pig, a Miss Piggy doll, a small ham, or sack of potatoes!

AN IRISH POTATO JIG

RIGGIDY HIGGIDY WIGGIDY RIG
PADDY DANCES AN IRISH JIG
WHILE FEEDING POTATOES TO HIS PIG
RIGGIDY HIGGIDY WIGGIDY RIG
OUT GOES YOU!

For anyone really into the spirit of Irish Jig, including you as host, consider a dramatic reading of the following poem, with a chorus provided for your "chorus" of guests. . . .

THE OULD IRISH JIG

My blessing be on you, ould Erin,
My own land of frolic and fun;
For all sorts of mirth and diversion,
Your like is not under the sun.
Bohemia may boast of her polka,

And Spain of her waltzes talks big;
Sure, they are all nothing but limping,
Compared with our ould Irish jig.

(Chorus)

> *Then a fig for your new-fashioned waltzes,*
> *Imported from Spain and from France;*
> *And a fig for the thing called polka—*
> *Our own Irish jig we will dance.*

I've heard how our jig came in fashion—
And believe that the story is true:
By Adam and Eve 'twas invented,
The reason was, partners were few.
And, though they could both dance the polka,
Eve thought it was not over-chaste;
She preferred our ould jig to be dancing—
And faith, I approve of her taste.

(Chorus)

> *Then a fig for your new-fashioned waltzes,*
> *Imported from Spain and from France;*
> *And a fig for the thing called polka—*
> *Our own Irish jig we will dance.*

The light-hearted daughters of Erin,
Like the wild mountain deer they can bound,
Their feet never touch the green island,
But music is struck from the ground.
And oft in the glens and green meadows,
The ould jig they dance with such grace,
That even the daisies they tread on,
Look up with delight in their face.

(Chorus)
>   *Then a fig for your new-fashioned waltzes,*
>   *Imported from Spain and from France;*
>   *And a fig for the thing called polka—*
>   *Our own Irish jig we will dance.*

An ould Irish jig, too, was danced by
The kings and the great men or yore;
King O'Toole could himself neatly foot it
To a tune they call *"Rory O'More."*
And oft in the great hall of Tara,
Our famous King Brian Boru
Danced an ould Irish jig with his nobles,
And played his own harp to them, too.

(Chorus)

> *Then a fig for your new-fashioned waltzes,*
> *Imported from Spain and from France;*
> *And a fig for the thing called polka—*
> *Our own Irish jig we will dance.*

And sure, when Herodias' daughter
Was dancing to King Herod's sight,
His heart that for years had been frozen
Was thawed with pure love and delight;
I've heard Father Flanagan tell,
'Twas our own Irish jig that she footed,
That pleased the ould villain so well.

(Chorus)

> *Then a fig for your new-fashioned waltzes,*
> *Imported from Spain and from France;*
> *And a fig for the thing called polka—*
> *Our own Irish jig we will dance.*

—James McKowen (1814-1889),
from *Joys of Irish Humor,*
by Henry D. Spalding.

The Leprechaun's
Pot O' Gold

The *Piece de Resistance*
(if you'll excuse my French(!)

For a mythical introduction to this game, refer
to the Glossary in the "Blarney" Chapter for
information on leprechauns. This shenanigan
requires original forethought in addition to
preparation. Directions are listed numerically.

1.   Decide what will be the Leprechaun's
Pot O' Gold: a bag of gold foil wrapped
chocolate coins, a sack of shinny pennies, a
brass pot filled with either of the above, or
other creative idea. Also needed is a small
stack of blank index cards.

2.   Weigh carefully where in the general
social area this Pot O' Gold could be hid.
Remember that you may have guests searching
in the area for potatoes, and you do not want
an inadvertent, premature discovery. Be aware
this hiding place must be made obscure, in
that *clues will direct the hunt*. Evaluate what
literal clues could be given, and what Irish

signs or symbols could be inconspicuously placed that will reflect the written clues and lead to finding the hidden treasure. The following format can be duplicated or adapted.

3.   Select several Irish Blessings dependent upon the number of participants (refer to the section on Irish Blessings). Write one verse or line of each blessing on one side of separate index cards, i.e., one verse or line per card.

FRONT OF INDEX CARDS	BACK OF INDEX CARDS
May the road rise up to meet you	A
May the wind be ever at your back	POCKET
May the sun shine warm upon your face	FULL
The rain fall soft upon your fields	OF
And until we meet again	GREEN

May God hold you in the palm of His hand	SHAMROCKS
May the good Lord	AN
take a liking to you,	IRISH
but not too soon!	BLESSING
I ask a leprechaun to bring	SOMEWHERE
A pot of gold to you,	OVER
I ask a fiddler if he'd play	THE
Your favorite ditty too,	RAINBOW
I ask the saints to walk with you	YOU
Each step along the way,	WILL
And now I'm asking you to have	FIND
A very happy day!	ME
Leprechauns, castles, good luck, laughter	AN

Lullabies, dreams and love ever after,	IRISH
Poems and songs with pipes and drums	COAT
A thousand welcomes when anyone comes,	OF
That's an Irish wish for you!	ARMS

These verses will be used to complete whole Irish Blessings, which in turn will reveal clues to the gold. On the back side of each index card, that is, on the back side of each written verse, you will write your clue, one word or phrase per card, in sequential order. A complete clue is revealed for each assembled blessing. Observe the above diagram of the index cards:

Get the picture? Index cards have a verse of Irish Blessing on each front side, and a word of the clue on each back side. From these four clues, can you guess where the Leprechaun's Pot O' Gold is in this scenario? Meanwhile, here's how to use the index cards to determine the clues for the gold.

The twenty-two index cards are shuffled and passed out among all participants, blessing side up. Participants mingle, attempting to reconstruct in proper sequence the complete Irish Blessing. When they assemble the Irish Blessing and turn it over, a clue is revealed. Four blessings yield four clues. From these clues, they set out to find the gold. You, as organizer, observe in amusement.

Now, in the scenario given, where *did* that Leprechaun hide his Pot O' Gold? Answer: In the foyer — beyond where the rainbow hangs — in the closet — next to the Irish Coat of Arms mounted above an Irish Blessing plaque — and in the pocket of an overcoat belonging to the Irish head of household(!) Faith and Begorrah, wasn't *that* easy to figure out?

Limerick Charades

Now may be the time to give friends center stage for their "loony limericks," but don't be surprised by a dearth of ingenuity as the limerick doesn't come easy when poets are distracted by comestibles and sweepstakes. Expect limericks of the past to be resurrected, and since the "innocence" of limericks has regressed through the years, sure'n likely what you'll hear will be bawdy! Beyond what friends come up with, here are some limericks to use in a game of charades. Adapt your own rules, but consider grouping friends in "twos" —giving each team a limerick card— allowing one person to read the *trite* words while the other person acts out the *demonstrative* words which you can copy on cards in bold print. . . .

Note that Section One limericks are bawdy favorites, appropriate for ADULTS, *and not all adults at that!* (Understand that these verses are of Irish origin, and not meant to offend.)   Section Two limericks are a mixed bag. Section Three poems are suitable for youth.

—.—.—.—.—.—.—.—.—.—.—.—

Section One:

On the chest of a barmaid of Sale
Were tattooed the prices of ale
        And on her behind
        For the sake of the blind
Was the same information in Braille.

—Anon

There was an old man in a trunk
Who inquired of his wife "am I drunk?"
        She replied with regret
        'I'm afraid so, my pet'
And he answered "It's just as I thunk!"

—Ogden Nash

Well, if it's a sin to like Guinness
Then that I admits what my sin is
    I like it with fizz
    Or just as it is,
And it's much better for me than gin is.

                —Cyril Ray

There was an old drunkard of Devon
Who died and ascended to heaven
    But he cried "This is Hades—
    There are no naughty ladies,
And pubs are all shut by eleven!

                —Ron Rubin

A naive young lady of Cork
Was told she was brought by the stork
    But after a day
    With a gent called O'Shea
She was doubtful of that sort of talk.

                —Reg Yearley

There was a young lady of Trent
Who said that she knew what it meant
   When men asked her to dine
   With cocktails and wine
She knew what it meant —but she went.

                —Anon

There was a young girl of St. Cyr
Whose reflex reactions were queer
   Her escort said "Mabel,
   Get up off the table,
That money is there for the beer!"

                —Anon

Said old father William "I'm humble
And getting too old for a tumble
   But produce me a blonde
   And I'm still not beyond
An attempt at an interesting fumble!"

            —Conrad Aiken

There was a young monk from Siberia
Whose morals were very inferior
    He did to a nun
    What he shouldn't have done
And now she's a mother superior.

                  —Anon

There once was a lass with such graces
That her curves cried aloud for embraces.
    "You look," said McGee,
    "Like a million to me,
Invested in all the right places.

                  —Anon

A colleen from old Londonderry,
On Guinness was loving and merry.
    She dallied with sin,
    On bourbon and gin,
But was rigid and frigid with sherry.

                  —Anon

Some verses like these, I surmise,
Were not meant for heavenly eyes.
 Saints Peter and Paul
 Don't get them at all,
And Our Father's aghast with surprise!

     —Anon

Section Two:

There was an old fellow of Trinity
A doctor well versed in divinity
 But he took to free thinking
 And then to deep drinking
And so had to leave the vicinity.

    —Arthur Clement Hilton

A blarneyin' bucko named Pat,
To girls he proposed this and that.
    When he spoke about "this"
    He meant cuddle and kiss,
But Lord knows what he meant by his "that."

—*Anon*

A lovely young rose of Tralee
Was naughty while out on a spree.
    Now she writes to the papers,
    Deploring such capers,
And signs herself, "Mother MacKree."

—*Anon*

"I've observed the bird and the bee,"
Said a sweet little rose of Tralee.
    "Their ways are so strange,
    I could never arrange
To let anyone try that with me."

—*Anon*

A bishop residing in Meath
Sat down on his set of false teeth'
Said he, with a start,
"O Lord, bless my heart!
I've bitten myself underneath!"

—*Anon*

There was a young priest of Dun Laoghaire
Who stood on his head in the Kyrie
When people asked why
He said in reply
"It's the latest liturgical theory."

—*Anon*

A studious colleen named Breeze,
Weighed down with BA's and MD's
Collapsed from the strain
Said her doctor, " 'Tis plain
You are killing yourself by degrees."

—*Anon*

God's plan made a hopeful beginning
But man spoilt his chances by sinning
> *We trust that the story*
> *Will end in great glory*
But at present the other side's winning.

—Anon

Section Three:

There was an old man with a flute
A serpent ran into his boot
> *But he played day and night*
> *Till the serpent took flight*
And avoided that man with a flute.

—Edward Lear

There was an old man of Dumbree
Who taught little owls to drink tea
  For he said, "To eat mice
  Is not very nice,"
That amiable man of Dumbree.

—Edward Lear

There was an old man with a beard,
Who said, "It's just as I feared!—
  Two owls and a hen,
  Four larks and a wren,
Have all built their nests in my beard!

—Edward Lear

There once were two cats of Kilkenny,
Each thought there was one cat too many;
  So they fought and they fit,
  and they scratched and they bit,
Till instead of two cats there weren't any.

—*Anon*

There was a young lady of Kent
Whose nose was most awfully bent.
 One day I suppose
 She followed her nose
For no one knew which way she went.

       —Anon

A diner while dining at Crew
Found quite a large mouse in his stew.
 Said the waiter, "Don't shout,
 And wave it about,
Or the rest will be wanting one too."

       —Anon

There was a young woman of Ayr,
Tried to steal out of church during prayer,
 But the squeak of her shoes
 So enlivened the pews
That she sat down again in despair.

       —Anon

There was a young farmer of Leeds
Who swallowed six packets of seeds.
  It soon came to pass
  He was covered with grass
And couldn't sit down for the weeds.

—*Anon*

There once was a pious young priest
Who lived almost wholly on yeast;
  "For," he said "it is plain
  We must all rise again,
And I want to get started at least."

—*Anon*

His sister named Lucy O'Finner
Grew constantly thinner and thinner,
  The reason was plain
  She slept out in the rain
And was never allowed any dinner.

—Lewis Carroll

Chapter Six

SKIT·TLES

as the old
cock crows,

the young
cock learns

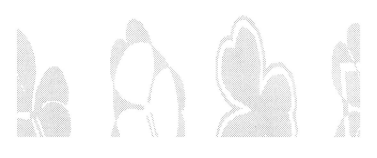

Sure 'n we've exhausted all creative ideas for this party? Begorrah, if there isn't more! So invite your friends to gather round, solicit or select volunteers, provide copies of these dramatic parts, and inspired by conviviality and spirits—

"Take One—

"Action!

"—Roll It!"

SURE DON'T YA KNOW

GIRL: Oh what's the smile for, Paddy boy,
                That goes from ear to ear?

PADDY: Sure don't ye know what day it is?
                Saint Patrick's Day is here!

BOY: And what' the green for, Paddy boy,
        the wearin' of th' green?

PADDY: It's tokening the Emerald Isle,
        The greenest place you've seen.

GIRL: And what's the shamrock, Paddy
        boy,
        With leaves that come in three?

PADDY: Why don't ye know that illustrates
        The Holy Trinity?

BOY: And what's the song for, Paddy boy,
        That sets the day apart?

PADDY: Tis just the Irish joy in me
        A burstin' from me' heart.

THE
DUBLIN PLAYERS
COMPANY

presents

"Alive, Alive-O"

Distinguished cast of characters—

Tricia . . . . .Rhonda CORNER

Waiter . . . . .Chuck ROAST

Scene: *A table at the Shamrock Restaurant*

TRICIA: Waiter — *oh, waiter!* Come quick! My husband just dropped dead!

WAITER: Hey, chef! There's something wrong again with the cockles and mussels!

PSHAW ON IRELAND, MR. LOCKE

JOHN LOCKE
(1847-1889)

O Ireland, isn't it grand you look?
Like a bride in her rich adornin';
And with all the pent-up love of my heart,
I bid you the top o' the mornin'!

BERNARD SHAW
(1856-1950)

At last I went to Ireland
'Twas raining cats and dogs:
I found no music in the glens,
Nor purple in the bogs.
And as for angels' laughter in
The smelly Liffey's tide —
Well, my Irish daddy said it,
But the dear old humbug lied.

SAINT PATRICK
and the SERPENT
Excerpted from
Holiday Programs for Boys and Girls,
by AILEEN FISHER.

Cast—
Narrator, Girl, Boy, Serpent, St. Patrick.

Props—
Be simple and creative as characters and dialogue dictate! Possibilities: Miter-like hat, crosier-like staff, cloak for Patrick; (Green) silky shirt or cover-all, skull cap or hat for Snake; and a "box" big enough to step into. Hat or wrap for Girl and Boy.

NARRATOR:

Saint Patrick drove the serpents out
of Ireland, so 'tis said. From here
and there and roundabout, from Cork
to Malin Head. He banished all the
snakes there were....

GIRL:
Except for one that wouldn't stir!

BOY:
Except for one that wouldn't leave!

ALL:
And sure it made Saint Patrick grieve.

NARRATOR:
Saint Patrick drove the serpents out of Ireland, so they claim. From here and there and roundabout, it brought Saint Patrick fame. He cast the serpents in the sea....

BOY:
Except for one that wouldn't flee!

GIRL:
Except for one that wouldn't drown!

ALL:
And sure it made Saint Patrick frown.

NARRATOR:
Saint Patrick was a canny man, a prudent man, they say; and so he conjured up a plan, he built a box-like

crate; and sweetly asked the serpent in. . . .

GIRL:

The serpent stroked its satin skin, and wouldn't try the box at all; but said. . . .

SERPENT:

For me, it's much too small.

NARRATOR:

Saint Patrick was a learned man, and subtle, so they tell. He coaxed the serpent. . . .

PATRICK:

Faith, you can fit very well; I'm sure you can, with room to spare.

SERPENT:

I can't, you know; I can't, so there.

PATRICK:

You can.

SERPENT:

I can't.

S⊤. P⊣⊤⊢⊏⊏ ⊣⊓⊐ ⊤⊢⊏ S⊓⊣⊏⊏⊒, by Shawn Van Briesen. 1996

PATRICK:
I know I'm right.

SERPENT:
You're wrong!

ALL:
They argued day and night.

NARRATOR:
Saint Patrick had a mighty voice,
persuasive, so they state; it made the
Emerald Isle rejoice to hear the great
debate....

PATRICK:
You'll fit the box.

SERPENT:
I won't at all.

PATRICK:
It's plenty big.

SERPENT:
It's pinchy small.

PATRICK:
Unless you prove it, I am right.

SERPENT:
I'll show you then, the box is tight!

NARRATOR:
*Saint Patrick watched the serpent glide
into the box, 'tis told, and when it
mostly was inside, the canny Saint made
bold, to close the lid and tie it tight, and
throw the box with all his might, upon
the waves that rolled away....*

ALL:
And sure it made Saint Patrick gay.

NARRATOR:
*Saint Patrick drove the serpents out
of Ireland, so 'tis said; he scoured the
country roundabout, from Cork to Malin
Head; and banished all the snakes there
were....*

GIRL:
Including one that wouldn't stir....

BOY:
Including one that left the isle, all boxed
and tied in state and style. . . .
ALL:
And sure it made Saint Patrick smile!

NARRATOR:
The End.

LEGEND OF THE BLARNEY STONE

(This original melodrama is a composite of
legends that surround the Blarney Stone.)

Characters—

Forlorn LAD *seeking love*

Helpful LEPRECHAUN

WICKLOW WITCH *indebted*

Lovely LASSIE *awaiting love*

Props—
As desired, or as inspired by the text

—·—·—·—·—·—·—·—·—

Setting—
A river glen not far from King McCarthy's
Castle in Blarney, County Cork. . . .

LAD:
She loves me—she loves me not—she
loves me—she loves me not—

LEPRECHAUN:
Hey laddie, why you sitting there,
looking so forlorn?

LAD:
Who are you, whose voice I hear, upon
this cloudy morn?

LEPRECHAUN:
Why, I'm your fairy leprechaun, and
you're near my fairy rath. I hope it's not
my crock of gold you're searching on
this path? Ah, but now I see and hear ye
lad, you're too distraught and torn. So
answer me my question, boy, why look
you so forlorn?

LAD:

I've not known a leprechaun to be a caring bloke, but trusting that you mean no harm, I'll tell you of my yoke. I love a pretty lassie, I love her as can be, but when I try to tell her so, she simply laughs at me. I can't express my love in words, nor sing a lover's ballad, and all professions of my love, have seemed to her invalid.

LEPRECHAUN:

Ha, that's no worry for me, lad, for I make mince of words. Of our romantic reputation, I am sure you've heard: I'd steal her away, is how I'd make my play. But tell me lad, does she love you? The truth now, yea or nay?

LAD:

I believe she does, old fairy man, for she giggles when she takes my hand. And touches my lips when I stutter to say: "how do I love thee, let's count the ways." But I'm afraid of loosin' her, this Tralee Rose a'bloomin', for she has

LAD (cont.)
other suitors, who I'm sure will come a
woo'in.

LEPRECHAUN:
Lad, your stuttering has touched my
mischievous heart, but my tricks and my
shenanigans are not a helpful start. So
let me light my pipe and think on this a
while. . . .

LASSIE [NARRATES]: *Heard from down
the river glen—*

WITCH:
HELP! HELP! I can't swim, I'm
frowning, frowning, frowning!
A curse upon you slippery rock, that
caused me this de-crowning.
Help me, oh you forces of nature, I'm
drowning, drowning, drowning!

LEPRECHAUN:
Hear ye and look, lad, why it's the
Wicklow Witch, likely hunting toads

for her magic potion pitch. She's
slipped upon the peat moss and fallen
in the river, it won't be long before the
deep, drags her down with ice cold
shivers.

LAD:
Well, aren't you going to do something,
wily Leprechaun. Your magic has the
power, you fairies have the braun.

LEPRECHAUN:
'Fraid not, lad, I'm a shoemaker, not a
swimmer. And when it comes to
witches in water, my power's even
dimmer. It's up to you to save the day,
"carpe diem" the witch would say!

WITCH:
HELP ME! HELP ME! I'm frowning,
drowning, shivering away. Carpe diem,
won't someone save the day!

LEPRECHAUN:
Foretold in truth, did I not say!

LAD:

Hold on there, Wicklow Witch— I'll
make a last ditch to save you!

LASSIE [NARRATES]:

The lad pulls the witch safely from the
water to the riverbank.... ("Oh, my
hero!")

WITCH:

Thank you, lad, you saved my life, this
good ol' witch is owing. And for such
mercy I repay, what favor now
bestowing?

LAD:

It was nothing, ma'am, and in return, I
ask nothing of your magic. Though
you're welcome nonetheless that I
spared you from the tragic.

LEPRECHAUN:

Now see here, lad, you're missin' your
chance; begorrah, don't refuse.... Hear,
Wicklow Witch, I'll tell you now, what
needs this man pursues— to win the
hand of the Las he loves, for he lacks

the words to say it.

WITCH:
Well just like you, ol' leprechaun, I have
no magic wand, to wave and make them
fall in love, sure 'n like two turtle doves.
But I know a secret I shall share, for
saving my dear life; so here's what you
need do, sad lad, to make your love-life
right—

On the domain of King McCarthy
Atop his cold stone tower
In the turret of Blarney Castle
There's a stone with magic power
Upon all fours do kiss the stone
And flattery becomes your own.

LASSIE [NARRATES]:
So our lad takes leave of the leprechaun
and witch, and goes off to find the
Blarney Stone. He finds it and kisses it,
in hope of receiving the gift of flattery,
which, in its exaggerated Irish form, has
come to be known as BLARNEY *—"He*
is my hero!"— he then returns to the
river glen....

LAD:
Leathercrafting Leprechaun, dear bloke,
where are you now? I know you're
'round here somewhere, for your pipe
smoke does abound, and beyond the
toadstool there, I hear your tapping
sound.

LEPRECHAUN:
Poof! See me now, lad, giddy as can
be, at the thought of your good fortune,
for which I envy thee.

LAD:
Aye, and with confidence to flatter and
the words to be loquacious, I am off to
win the heart and hand of my fair lady
gracious. And inviting you to come
along, my lithesome leprechaun.

LEPRECHAUN:
And proud I'd be to follow you, and
leap along so stealthy; to steal a glance
of requited love, would be for me so
healthy; though more than love I do
prefer that nature make me wealthy!

LASSIE:
I see a handsome lad approaches
. . . . *"My hero come at last!"*

LAD:
Top o' the mornin' to you, my lovely
colleen, with eyes of blue, though shall
"I" commend the day to you, so filled
with grace and beauty true?
Rather—

"Shall I compare thee to a summer's day?
Thou art more lovely and more temperate:
Rough winds do shake the darling buds of May,
And summer's lease hath all too short a date:
So long as men can breathe, or eyes can see,
So long lives love, and this gives life to thee."

LASSIE:
Faith and begorrah, my friend, if
you're not in a fine mood this morn, so
confident and flattering in every word
you've worn. Sure 'n I sense there is no
end, a proposal's to be born. . .
(whisperingly) *"My Hero."*

LAD:

True, my flame of heart's desire, and words I shall not tarry, for I have come to ask your hand, I wish with thee to marry.

LASSIE:

Sure 'n wouldn't I be honored, to accept your loving offer, for its days and weeks I've longed to hear, these courtly words be proffered.

LEPRECHAUN [NARRATES]:

And so the lad, for his saving deed
knowledge of the Blarney Stone
received whose magic power to flatter
his wife (and many others) throughout
his life brought him happiness all his
years.

Now—

Legend of the Blarney Stone soon spread
people seeking its magic charms are led
to kiss the stone and claim its flattery
but what I hear them say 'round me
sounds more and more like pure blarney,
Aye, and that is what it's come to be!

TALE OF THE
HAUNTED CASTLE

This improvisational story invites partici-
pation of an imaginary sort with a young
audience. Tell it in the mood of a ghost story,
if you will. Set the stage for the youngsters to
contribute their dramatic sounds, build the
mental picture of the castle, and allow your
young listeners to sound out their parts and to
give their own lines to the poem.

Out on the Irish moorland, amidst moss
and heather and ferns,

there stands an empty, cold, stone castle

built during the medieval age of Ireland
a long time ago.

Tapestries and Coats of Arms hung
on its gray stone walls;

candles glowed and torches burned

in its dark rooms and halls and stairwells.

Lords and ladies, knights and squires,

bishops and priests, minstrels and poets,

servants and common folk dwelt in this abode.

Now the fortress is deserted, parts crumbled
to the ground.

But once a year, on March 17, the folks in
towns nearby,

say they hear the strangest sounds,
on St. Patrick's Day...

Can you imagine what they hear?

[here the audience imagines the castle's haunting
sounds, calling them out in turn, or you can lead
them to the sounds they make by these keys
words.]

The drawbridge....
In the courtyard....
Through the tower window....

In the great banquet hall....
From the harp....
Down in the dungeon....
Lords and Ladies....
Knights....
Bishops....
Minstrels....
Poets....
and Servants....
while St. Patrick himself is heard to say....

We'll never know if this ghostly tale
of the Irish castle is true,

unless we visit Ireland on Saint Patrick's
Day of due,

but herein played a chance for you to imagine
what passed through!

EIRE IMPRESSIONS

This next poem is an original piece by the author upon visiting Ireland a second time in 1991, and may serve as visualization for a drawing contest titled: "Picture Ireland"

(Teachers may wish to play softly a tape
of Irish music while reciting the poem.)

Erie Impressions—

Countryside of rolling hills

a checkerboard of all shapes square

a patchwork quilt of all shades green

patterns, parcels, pastures

stitched by low stone walls and

dotted with gumdrop buttons
of piled golden hay.

Blue sky heaven

today awash in cloud navy gray

stretching-extending-horizontally seaward

casting shadows across forest green fields

raindrops retreating before the rainbow waves

a flag of promise for tomorrow.

Cubic flatface houses stone painted white

roofs thatched brown with weathered hay or

contemporized peat brown earthen tile over

black-framed windows
and doors squarely placed

looking, sounding, like eyes and mouth

bidding "failte" to this green-shamrocked
B&B.

Roads by all counts country narrow

lined, defined by block rock fences or

thick green wild shrub hedges

scratching, brushing two cars passing

where cows and sheep escape pasture grass

and rest their hoofs on pavement's path

impeding passersby with
cold stares of big brown eyes.

Distant castle towers crumbled cold

ancient abbey walls stand angular alone

Celtic crosses amass in rank and file

in cemetery town or empty field,

monumental remnants of a medieval past

glorious history of man (and England)

called to faith today by Church belfries

fingerpointing skyward.

Maloney's, O'Fallon's, and Kelly's,

Clancy's, O'Brien's, and Flynn's,
Pubs front every village street

plain unobtrusive facades quietly disguising

an inner world of Gaelic mirth and blarney

to which Arthur Guinness hangs his black

and orange seal—a frothy pint o' *"Slainte"*.

Irish folk everyman everywhere

drabbed in threadworn woolens

dark earthly colored clothes

armored elements of time and weather

contending life slow and simple

counting blessings of family, friends and dog

warm smile on faces red freckled worn

quick ta' quiver a quip in brogue

with a leprechaun's twinkle of eye.

Eire impresses as Ireland beckons

one back to "cead mille failte",

to the land of our ancestors

to a time of man's rootedness

in earth and sky and Destiny.

The Celtic Connection

What seems to bind many Irish Americans to Eire is captured in this poem by Charles "Charlie" Kidney given (for tips) to passersby from his perch on a street corner in Cork—

A blast of Celtic music,
A sound fossil from the past,
Carried from a distant space
To ear, through mouth,
Through millennium of time,
Tied his soul to a billion men,
Of the same tribe,
Of the same spirit,
By some intangible thread.

THE "WEE PEOPLE"

The "Wee People" represent the creatures of the Irish spirit world. There are trooping fairies who dance in the forests and by the rivers. You can tell their presence by the rustling of leaves and the sighing of wind.

There are leprechauns or fairy shoemakers, old, withered, solitary fellows. These creatures always have an eye for mischief, especially for a pretty girl whom he does not mind stealing away for his own. They are believed to have a crock of gold hidden away which can also be used as ransom should they ever be caught, though leprechauns are also known to lure others into their indentured service by tempting humans with such golden wealth.

Several fairy spirits are distinguished—

❂ The *clurichaun* makes himself at home in wine cellars, a leprechaun on a spree....

❀ The *pooka* can take the form of many animals and can foretell the future, provided you are careful to please the creature in everything you say and do. . . .

❀ The *banshee* is a dark and ghostly fairy who attends old Irish families to wail outside the house when death is near. . . .

These *deenee shee* are believed to be the former gods of pagan Ireland, the *Tuatha De Danan,* who diminished in size after their divine displacement by the Christian religion. Many consider these "fairies" as fallen angels, not good enough to be saved nor bad enough to be damned.

The fairies are quick to take offense and must be addressed or mentioned in a respectful manner. The peasantry of old spoke of them in whispers or not at all, and when so, referred to them as "the good people" though they were not always good. But fairies have their merry side too, enjoying music and song, good food and drink. (Parts of the proceeding have been paraphrased from Henry Spalding.)

The following *Tales of the "wee people"* can be read or memorized for storytelling, or acted out in a skit as the following one has been adapted.

_____

THE PRIEST'S SUPPER
(Adapted from *Fairy Legends and Traditions of the South of Ireland,* Thomas Crofton Croker, 1828. Printed full in *Joys of Irish Humor,* by Henry D. Spalding)

Once on a bright moonlit evening, there was a merry troop of fairies —dancing and playing all manner of pranks. The scene of their merriment was not far distant from a poor village in west County Cork. However, as the fairies can have everything they want for wishing, poverty does not trouble them much.

By the river side the little fellows were dancing in a ring as gaily as may be, with their red caps wagging about at every bound. Thus did they carry on until one of them chirped out—

> "Cease, cease your drumming,
> Here's an end to our mumming;
> > *By my smell*
> > *I can tell*
> A priest this way is coming!"

And away every one of the fairies scampered, concealing themselves under leaves of green; some hiding behind stones, others under the river bank in holes and crannies.

The fairy speaker was not mistaken, for along the road came Father Horrigan, thinking to himself that it was so late he would make an end of his journey at the first cabin he came to. So he stopped at the dwelling of Dermod Leary, lifted the latch and entered with, "My blessing on all here."

Now Father Horrigan was a welcome guest wherever he went, for no man was more pious

or beloved; and it was a great trouble to
Dermod that he had nothing to offer His
Reverence except the potatoes which "the
woman" had boiling in a pot over the fire. He
thought of the net he had set in the river, but
the chances were against his finding a fish in
it. *"No matter,"* thought Dermod, *"there can
be no harm in stepping down to see."*

Down to the riverside went Dermod, and he
found in the net as fine a salmon as ever
jumped in bright waters. But as he was going
to take it out, the net was pulled from him —
he could not tell how or by whom— and away
got the salmon, swimming gaily down stream.

Dermod looked sorrowfully at the wake which
the fish had left in the moonlit water, and then
with an angry motion of his hand and a stamp
of his foot, he gave vent to his feelings: "May
bitter bad luck attend you night and day,
salmon, wherever you go! You ought to be
ashamed to give me the slip like that. And I'm
clear in my mind you'll come to no good, for
some kind of evil thing helped you. Did I
not feel it pull the net, strong as the devil

himself?"

"That's not true," said one of the little fairies with a throng of companions at his heels. "There was only a dozen of us pulling against you."

Dermod gazed with wonder on the tiny speaker who continued: "Make yourself no-ways uneasy about the priest's supper, for if you ask him one question from us, there will be as fine a supper before him as ever was spread on a table."

"I'll have nothing to do with you," replied Dermod. "I know better than to sell myself to the likes of you for a supper; and more than that, I know Father Horrigan has more regard for my soul than to wish me to pledge it forever."

The little speaker persisted, "Will you ask the priest one civil question for us?"

Dermod considered for some time, and thought that no harm could come of asking a civil question. "I see no objection to that," said Dermod, "but I'll have nothing to do with your supper— mind that."

"Then," said the little fairy while the rest came crowding after, "go and ask Father Horrigan to tell us whether our souls will be saved at the last day, like the souls of good Christians."

Away went Dermod to his cabin, where he found the potatoes placed out on the table, his good woman handing the biggest of them over to Father Horrigan.

"Please, Your Reverence," said Dermod, "may I make bold to ask Your Honor one question?"

"What may that be?" said Father Horrigan.

"Why, begging Your Reverence's pardon, it is if the souls of 'the good people' are to be saved at the last day."

"Who bid you ask me that question, Leary?" said the priest sternly.

"I'll tell no lies about the matter—" said Dermod. "It was the good people themselves who sent me to ask; there are thousands down on the river bank, waiting for me to go back with the answer."

"Go back by all means," said the priest, "and tell them if they want to know, to come here to me themselves, and I'll answer any question they are pleased to ask, with the greatest pleasure."

Dermod returned to the fairies, who came swarming around him to hear what the priest had said. Dermod spoke out like the bold man he was. But when they heard that they must go to the priest, away they fled, whisking by poor Dermod so fast he was quite bewildered.

When he came to himself, he went back to his cabin, and ate his lone potato along with Father Horrigan who made quite light of the matter. But Dermod could not help thinking that His Reverence, whose words had the power to banish the fairies, could not have used his power to get back the fine fat salmon that "the good people" had taken away from him. For Dermod's mouth watered at the thought of what dinner might have been, while that fine fat salmon swam gaily down the stream!

_._.._.._.._.._.._.._.._.._.._.._.._.._.._.

MASTER AND MAN
(This old folk legend is adapted as a dramatic reading for three thespian orators and one "lady-like soft sneezer.")

READERS:
>Narrator (NAR)
>Billy MacDaniel (BMD)
>The Little Man (TLM)
>Bridget Rooney (to sneeze, "lady-like")

NAR: *Now Billy MacDaniel was as likely a young man as ever shook his brogue during a patron (a festival held in honor of some patron saint), emptied a quart, or handled a shillelagh; fearing nothing but the lack of a drink; caring for nothing but who should pay; and thinking of nothing but how to have fun*

NAR (cont.)
over it. It so happened that Billy was going home one clear, frosty night not long after Christmas and felt pinched with cold. He chattered:

BMD: By my word, a drop of liquor would be no bad thing to keep a man's soul from freezing; and I wish I had a full measure of the best right now.

TLM: Never wish it twice, Billy.

NAR: *Said a little man in a three-cornered hat, bound with gold lace, and with great silver buckles on his shoes so big it was a wonder he could walk. And he held out a glass as big as himself, filled with as good a liquor as lips ever tasted.*

BMD: Success, my little fellow. Here's to your health, and thank you kindly, no matter who pays for the drink.

NAR: *And he took the glass and drained it to the very bottom without ever taking a second to breathe.*

TLM: Success, and your heartily welcome, Billy. But don't think to cheat me as you have done others. Out with your purse and pay me like a gentleman.

BMD: I pay you? Why, could I not take you up and put you in my pocket as easily as a blackberry?

TLM: Bedad, Billy MacDaniel! For your remarks, you shall be my servant for seven years and a day, and that is the way I will be paid. So make ready to follow me.

NAR: *When Billy heard this he began to feel sorry for having used such bold words toward the little man, and he felt himself obliged to follow him all the livelong night about the country. When morning began to dawn, the little man turned 'round to him and said—*

TLM: You may go home, Billy, but on your peril, don't fail to meet me in the Fort-field tonight. If you don't, it will be worse for you

TLM (cont.)
in the long run. If I find you a good servant,
you will find me an indulgent master.

NAR: *The next evening Billy was in the Fort-
field, and he was not there long before the
little man came along.*

TLM: Billy, I want you to saddle one of my
horses, we are going on a long journey tonight.
And you may saddle another for yourself—
you may be tired after your walking about last
night.
NAR: *Billy thought this very considerate of his
master, and thanked him accordingly; but
said—*

BMD: If I may be so bold, sir, I would ask
which is the way to your stable, for not a thing
do I see here but the fort, an old thorn tree, and
the stream at the bottom of the hill, with a bit
of the bog.

TLM: Ask no questions, Billy, but go over to
that bit of bog and bring me two of the
strongest bulrushes you can find.

NAR: *Billy did so, wondering what the little man was up to. He picked two of the stoutest rushes he could find, and brought them back to his master. Straddling one of the rushes between his short legs, the little man said—*

TLM: Get up now, Billy.

BMD: Where shall I get up, please Your Honor?

TLM: Why, upon horseback, like me, to be sure.

BMD: Is it making a fool of me, you'd be? Bidding me get on horseback, upon this bit of rush? Maybe you want to persuade me that this bulrush is a horse?

TLM: Up! Up! And no words. The best horse you ever rode was but a fool to this steed.

NAR: *So Billy, thinking all this was a joke, and fearing to vex his master, straddled the rush.*

TLM: Borram! Borram!

NAR: *Cried the little man (which in English means "to become great"). And presently the rushes swelled up into fine horses, and away they went at full speed. But Billy, having put the rush between his legs without minding how he did it, found himself sitting backwards on the horse, facing the horse's rump. And so quickly had his steed started off that he had no power to turn 'round, and there was nothing for him to hold on to but its tail. Alas, they came to their journey's end, and stopped at the gate of a fine house.*

TLM: Now, Billy, do as you see me do, and follow me close. But as you did not know your horse's head from his tail, mind that your own head does not spin round until you can't tell whether you are standing on your head or your heels.

NAR: *The little man then said some queer kind of words, and into the fine house they passed —through the keyhole of a door, and through one keyhole after another— until they were into the wine cellar, where the little man and*

Billy fell to drinking hard as could be.

BMD: The best of masters are you, surely, and well pleased will I be in your service if you continue to provide plenty of such drink!

TLM: I have made no bargain with you, and will make none; but up and follow me.

NAR: *And thus did they go on night after night, until there was not a gentleman's wine cellar in all Ireland they had not visited... Now one night when Billy MacDaniel met the little man as usual, and was going to fetch the rushes* —er, horses *for their journey, his master said to him—*

TLM: Billy, I shall want another horse tonight, for we may bring back more company than we take.

NAR: *So Billy, who knew better than to question any order given to him by his master, brought a third rush, much wondering who it might be that would travel back with them... Well away they went, Billy leading the third*

NAR (cont.)

horse, and they never stopped until they came to a snug farmer's house in County Limerick, close under the old castle that was built by the great king Brian Boru. Within the house there was a great carousing going on, and the little man stopped outside to listen. Then turning round he said—

TLM: Billy, I will be a thousand years old tomorrow.

BMD: "God bless us", sir, will you now?

TLM: O-chone! Don't ever say those words again, Billy, or you will be my ruin forever. Now Billy, as I will be a thousand years old tomorrow, I think it's full time for me to get married. And to that purpose have I come all the way here, for in this house, this very night, is young Darby Riley to be married to Bridget Rooney; and as she is tall and comely and of decent people, I think to marry the girl myself, and take her off with me.

BMD: And what will Darby Riley say to that?

TLM: Silence! I did not bring you here to ask questions.

NAR: *So without further argument, they passed through the keyhole as free as air, until they perched themselves upon the big beams which went across the house, overlooking the company below. The little man could not have sat more contentedly. They were both, master and man, looking down upon the fun that was going on. Under them were the priest and piper, the father of Darby Riley and his two brothers. There, too, were the proud father and mother of Bridget Rooney, her four sisters, three brothers, and uncles and aunts to make a full house of it. Plenty was there to eat and drink.*

Now it happened that just as Mrs. Rooney had helped his Reverence to the first cut of the pig's head, the bride gave a sneeze [Bridget sneezes softly], *which made everyone at the table start, but not a soul said, "God Bless Us", all thinking that the priest would have done so, but unfortunately his mouth was filled with pig's*

NAR (cont.)
head. So after a pause, the fun and merriment went on without the pious benediction.

Now the little man, throwing one leg from under him in a joyous flourish, his eye twinkling with a strange light, his eyebrows elevated into Gothic arches, exclaimed—

TLM: *Ha! Ha! Ha!* I have half of her now, surely. Let her sneeze but twice more, and she is mine, in spite of priest, mass book, and Darby Riley!

NAR: *Again the fair Bridget sneezed* [Bridget sneezes gently]*, but it was so gently, and she blushed so, that few except the little man seemed to take notice. No one thought of saying, "God Bless Us".*

All this time, Billy regarded the poor girl with sympathy, and could not help thinking what a terrible thing it was for a nice girl of nineteen, with large blue eyes, soft skin and dimpled cheeks, filled with health and joy, to be obliged to marry an ugly little man who was a thousand years old, barring a day.

Now, at this critical moment, the bride gave a third sneeze [Bridget sneezes], *and Billy roared out with all his might—*

BMD: "God Save Us!"

NAR: *No sooner was it uttered than the little man, his face glowing with rage and disappointment, sprang from the beam, and with the shrill of a cracked bagpipe, shrieked—*

TLM: I discharge you from my service, Billy MacDaniel —take THAT for your wages. . . .

NAR: *And he gave Billy a most furious kick in his butt, which sent his unfortunate servant sprawling down upon his face and hands, right into the middle of the supper table below.*

Now if Billy was astonished, imagine how much more was everyone of the company into which he was thrown. But when they heard his story, Father Cooney laid down his knife and

NAR (concludes)

fork, and married the young couple with all speed. And Billy MacDaniel danced the Rinka jig at their wedding, and plenty did he drink too, which was what he enjoyed more than dancing!

(Preceding skit adapted from Thomas Crofton Croker, 1828, Op. cit.. Printed full in "Spalding.")

Chapter Seven

SING·A·LONG

the older the fiddle
the sweeter the tune

The conclusion of dinner, or winding-down of the evening, is a fitting time to pass around song sheets and enjoin everyone in a nostalgic salute to Erin, and sentimental memory of loves past.

When Irish Eyes Are Smiling

Words by Chauncey Olcott and George Graff, Jr.;
Music by Ernest R. Ball; 1912

There's a tear in your eye, and I'm
wondering why,

for it never should be there at all.

With such pow'r in your smile,
sure a stone you'd beguile,

So there's never a tear-drop should fall.

When your sweet lilting laughter's
like some fairy song,

And your eyes twinkle bright as can be;

You should laugh all the while
and all other times smile,

and now smile a smile for me.

CHORUS—
>   When Irish eyes are smiling,
>   Sure it's like a morn in Spring.
>   In the lilt of Irish laughter
>   You can hear the angels sing.
>   When Irish hearts are happy,
>   All the world seems bright and gay,
>   And when Irish eyes are smiling,
>   Sure they steal your heart away.

For your smile is a part of
the love in your heart,

And it makes even sunshine
more bright.

Like the linnet's sweet song, crooning
all the day long,

Comes your laughter so tender and light.

For the springtime of life is
the sweetest of all,
there is ne'er a real care or regret;

And while springtime is ours
throughout all of youth' hours,

Let us smile each chance we get.

REPEAT CHORUS—
When Irish eyes are smiling,
Sure it's like a morn in Spring.
In the lilt of Irish laughter
You can hear the angels sing.
When Irish hearts are happy,
All the world seems bright and gay,
And when Irish eyes are smiling,
Sure they steal your heart away.

Molly Malone (Cockles and Mussels)

Words & Music: Anon; *circa* 1850.

In Dublin's fair city where
the girls are so pretty,

'Twas there I first met with
sweet Molly Malone;

She drove a wheelbarrow,
thro' streets broad and narrow,

Crying: "Cockles and mussels—
alive, alive all."

CHORUS—

Alive, Alive, O!
Alive, Alive, O!
Crying "Cockles and mussels—
alive, alive all."

She was a fishmonger, and
that was the wonder,

Her father and mother
were fishmongers too;

They drove wheelbarrows,

through streets broad and narrow,

Crying: "Cockles and mussels—
alive, alive all."

REPEAT CHORUS—
Alive, Alive, O!
Alive, Alive, O!
Crying "Cockles and mussels—
alive, alive all."

She died of the fever, and
nothing could save her,

And that was the end
of sweet Molly Malone;

But her ghost drives a barrow,
through streets broad and narrow,

Crying: "Cockles and mussels—
alive, alive all."

REPEAT CHORUS—
Alive, Alive, O!
Alive, Alive, O!
Crying "Cockles and mussels—
alive, alive all."

Too-Ra-Loo-Ra-Loo-Ral (That's An Irish Lullaby)

Words & Music by James Royce Shannon; 1913.

Over in Killarney,

Many years ago,

Me Mother sang a song to me

in tones so sweet and low,

Just a simple little ditty,
in her good ould Irish way,

And I'd give the world if she
could sing that song to me this day.

CHORUS—

Too-ra-loo-ra-loo-ral, too-ra-loo-ra-li,
Too-ra-loo-ra-loo-ral, Hush now don't you cry!
Too-ra-loo-ra-loo-ral, Too-ra-loo-ra-li,
Too-ra-loo-ra-loo-ral, That's an Irish lullaby.

Oft, in dreams, I wander

To that cot again,

I feel her arms a huggin' me

as when she held me then.

And I hear her voice a hummin'
to me as in days of yore,

When she used to rock me
fast asleep outside the cabin door.

REPEAT CHORUS—

Too-ra-loo-ra-loo-ral, too-ra-loo-ra-li,
Too-ra-loo-ra-loo-ral, Hush now don't you cry!
Too-ra-loo-ra-loo-ral, Too-ra-loo-ra-li,
Too-ra-loo-ra-loo-ral, That's an Irish lullaby.

The Londonderry Air (O Danny Boy)

Words & Music: Anon; *circa* 1850.

Oh, Danny Boy, the pipes, the pipes are calling
From glen to glen, and down the mountain side,
The summer's gone, and all the roses falling,
It's you, it's you must go, and I must bide.

But come ye back, when summer's in the meadow,

Or when the valley's hushed and white with snow,

It's I'll be here, in sunshine or in shadow,

Oh Danny Boy, oh Danny Boy, I love you so!

But when ye come, and all the flowers are dying,

And I am dead, as dead I well may be,

Ye'll come and find the place where I am lying,

And kneel and say an Ave there for me.

Cover to the sheet music for the "Fred E. Weatherly" version of DANNY BOY, circa 1913.

And I shall hear, though soft you tread above me,

And all my grave will warmer, sweeter be,

For you will bend and tell me that you love me,

And I shall sleep in peace until you come to me!

Oh, Danny Boy, the pipes, the pipes are calling
From glen to glen, and down the mountain side,
The summer's gone, and all the roses falling,
It's you, it's you must go, and I must bide.

The Wearin' Of The Green

Words by Dion Boucicault; Music: Anon; 1845.

Oh, Paddy dear, and did ye hear
the news that's goin' round?

The Shamrock is forbid by law
to grow on Irish ground,

St. Patrick's Day no more we'll keep;
his color can't be seen,

For there's a bloody law agin'
the Wearin o' the Green;

I met with Napper Tandy and he
tuk me by the hand,

And he said "how's poor ould Ireland,
and how now does she stand?

She's the most distressful country
that ever you have seen:

They're hanging men and women
there for "Wearin o' the Green."

— ·— ·— ·— ·— ·— ·—

Then since the color we must wear
is England's cruel red,

Sure Ireland's sons will ne'er forget
the blood that they have shed;

You may take the Shamrock from your
hut, and cast it on the sod,

But 'twill take root and flourish
still tho' under foot 'tis trod;

When the law can stop the blades of
grass from growing as they grow,

And when the leaves in summer-time
their verdure dare not show;

Then I will change the color
that I wear in my corbeen,

But 'till that day, please God, I'll stick to
"Wearin o' the Green."

— · — · — · — · — · — · — · — · — · —

But if at last our color should be
torn from Ireland's heart,

Her sons with shame and sorrow
from the dear old soil will part;

I've heard whisper of a country
that lies far beyant the say,

Where rich and poor stand equal,
in the light of freedom's day,

Oh Erin must we leave you,
driven by the tyrant's hand,

Must we ask a Mother's welcome
from a strange but happier land?

Where the cruel cross of England's
thraldom never shall be seen,

And where thank God we'll live and die
still "Wearin o' the Green."

My Wild Irish Rose

Words & Music by Chauncey Olcott; 1899.

If you listen, I'll sing you
a sweet little song

of a flower that's now
drooped and dead,

Yet dearer to me, yes,
than all of its mates,

tho' each holds aloft it proud head.

'Twas given to me by a girl that I know;

since we've met, faith, I've known
no repose,

She is dearer by far than the world's
brightest star,

and I call her my wild Irish Rose.

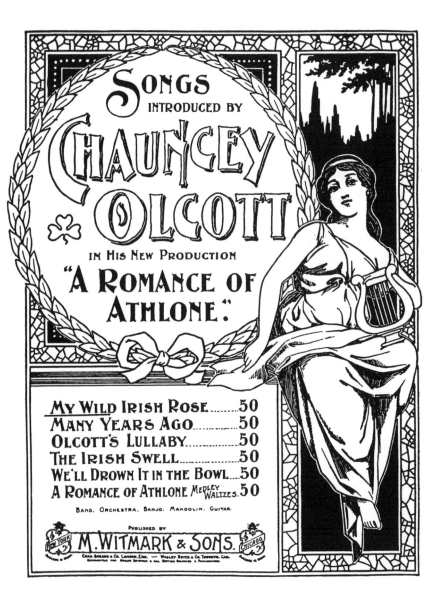

CHORUS—

My wild Irish Rose,
The sweetest flow'r that grows,
You may search ev'rywhere but none can compare
with my wild Irish Rose.
My wild Irish Rose, the dearest flow'r that grows
And some day for my sake, she may let me take
the bloom from my wild Irish Rose.

They may sing of their roses which,
by other names,

Would smell just as sweetly, they say,

But I know that my Rose
would never consent

to have that sweet name taken away.

Her glances are shy whene'er I pass by

the bower, where my true love grows;

And my one wish has been that

some day I may win

the heart of my wild Irish Rose.

REPEAT CHORUS—

My wild Irish Rose,
The sweetest flow'r that grows,
You may search ev'rywhere but none can compare
with my wild Irish Rose.
My wild Irish Rose, the dearest flow'r that grows
And some day for my sake, she may let me take
the bloom from my wild Irish Rose.

Mother Machree

(MACHREE means "my heart" or "my dear")
Words by Rida Johnson Young; Music by Chauncey
Olcott & Ernest R. Ball; 1910.

There's a spot in me heart which
no colleen may own,

There's a depth in me soul never
sounded or known,

There's a place in my mem'ry, my life,
that you fill,

No other can take it, no one ever will.

CHORUS—
Sure, I love the dear silver that shines in your hair
And the brow that's all furrowed
and wrinkled with care
I kiss the dear fingers so toil worn for me
Oh, God bless you and keep you, Mother Machree.

I'll Take You Home Again, Kathleen

Words & Music by Thomas P. Westendorf, 1876.

I'll take you home again, Kathleen,
Across the ocean wild and wide,

To where your heart has ever been,
Since first you were my bonny bride.

The roses all have left your cheek,
I've watched them fade away and die;

Your voice is sad when e'er you speak,
And tears be-dim your loving eyes.

CHORUS—

Oh! I will take you back, Kathleen,
To where your heart will feel no pain,
And when the fields are fresh and green,
I'll take you to your home again.

I know you love me, Kathleen dear,
Your heart was ever fond and true;

I always feel when you are near,
That life holds nothing dear but you.

The smiles that once you gave to me,

I scarcely ever see them now,

Tho' many, many times I see,
A dark'ning shadow on your brow.

CHORUS—

Oh! I will take you back, Kathleen,
To where your heart will feel no pain,
And when the fields are fresh and green,
I'll take you to your home again.

To that dear home beyond the sea,
My Kathleen shall again return,

And when thy old friends welcome thee,
Thy loving heart will cease to yearn.

Where laughs the little silver stream,
Beside your mother's humble cot,

And brightest rays of sunshine gleam,
There all your grief will be forgot.

CHORUS—

Oh! I will take you back, Kathleen,
To where your heart will feel no pain,
And when the fields are fresh and green,
I'll take you to your home again.

Chapter Eight
IRISH BLESSINGS

every tide
has an ebb

save the
tide of graces

Irish Blessings: Being a religious country and people (due greatly to Saint Patrick and his descendant disciples), the Irish are well known for their blessings —a mixture of traditional faith, wisdom, and folklore— touching on superstition and simple well-wishes. Many blessings have been adapted from the Great Prayer, which has come to be called the *Breastplate of Saint Patrick,* also referred to as the *Lorica.*

BREASTPLATE OF SAINT PATRICK

I arise today
through the strength of heaven:
Light of sun,
Radiance of moon,
Splendor of fire,
Speed of lightning,
Swiftness of wind,
Depth of sea,
Stability of rock.

I arise today
Through God's strength to pilot me:
God's might to uphold me,
God's wisdom to guide me,
God's eye to look before me,
God's ear to hear me,
God's word to speak for me,
God's hand to guard me,
God's way to lie before me,
God's shield to protect me,
God's host to save me,
From snares of devils,
From temptation of vices,
From everyone who wishes me ill
Afar and anear
Alone and in a multitude.

I summon today all these powers between
me and those evils:
Against every cruel merciless power that
may oppose my body and soul;
Against incantations of false prophets,

Against black laws of Pagandom,
Against false laws of heretics,
Against craft of idolatry,
Against spells of women and smiths
and wizards,
Against every knowledge that corrupts
man's body and soul.

Christ to shield me today
Against poison, against burning,
Against drowning, against wounding,
So that there may come to me abundance
of reward.

Christ with me, Christ before me,
Christ behind me,
Christ in me, Christ beneath me,
Christ above me,
Christ on my right hand, Christ
on my left,
Christ when I lie down, Christ
when I sit down,
Christ when I arise,

*Christ in the heart of every man
who thinks of me,
Christ in the mouth of everyone
who speaks of me,
Christ in every eye that sees me,
Christ in every ear that hears me.*

*I arise today through a mighty strength,
The invocation of the Trinity:
Through belief in the Threeness,
Through confession of the Oneness
Of the Creator of Creation.*

One can observe from this "God-filled" prayer of Patrick his own reliance on the power of God in his missionary work, the great dangers, threats and challenges he faced from a primitive pagan people. Finally, one can recognize those elementary elements which have become the essence of Irish blessings from ages past through ages present.

❧ IRISH BLESSINGS ❧

May the love and protection
Saint Patrick can give
Be yours in abundance
As long as you live.

May you have all the happiness
And luck that life can hold,
And at the end of all your rainbows
May you find a pot o' gold.

May the good saints protect you
And bless you today,
And may trouble ignore you
Each step of the way.

God grant me a sense of humor, Lord,
The saving grace to see a joke,
To win some happiness from life,
And pass it on to other folk.

May you always have these blessings,,,,
A soft breeze when summer comes,
A warm fireside in winter,
And always the warm soft smile of a friend.

> *May good luck be with you*
> *wherever you go,*
> *And blessings outnumber*
> *the shamrocks that grow.*

May trouble be less
And your blessings be more,
And nothing but happiness
Come through your door.

> *May good luck be your friend*
> *In whatever you do,*
> *And may trouble be always*
> *A stranger to you.*

May the lilt of Irish laughter

Lighten every load,

May the mist of Irish magic

Shorten every road,

May you taste the sweetest pleasures

That fortune ere bestowed,

And may all your friends remember

All the favors you are owed!

May this home and all therein

Be blessed with God's love.

May the grace of God's protection

And his great love abide

Within your home —

Within the hearts

Of all who dwell inside.

❀TOASTS ❀

To Drink to Health—
We will drink this drink
As Patrick would drink it
Full of grace and spilling over,
without fighting or quarreling or hint of shame,
or knowing that we will last until tomorrow.

To St. Patrick—
Saint Patrick was a gentleman
who through strategy and stealth
drove all the snakes from Ireland,
Here's a toasting to his health!

But not too many toastings
lest you lose yourself and then
forget the good Saint Patrick
and see all those snakes again!

To Ireland—

Here's to dear old Erin, that lovely Emerald Isle—
Here's to every colleen, and every colleen's smile—
Here's to Irish laughter, and "the little people" too—
Here's to dear old Erin, but most of all—here's to you!

To Good Wishes—
Health and long life to you
The wife of your choice to you
A child every year to you
Land without rent to you
And may you be half-an-hour in heaven
before the devil knows you're dead!

May you be poor in misfortune,
rich in blessings,
slow to make enemies,
quick to make friends.
But rich or poor,
quick or slow,
may you know nothing but happiness
from this day forward.

To Irish Whiskey—

Here is to Irish, a whiskey with heart,
that's smooth as a leprechaun's touch,
yet as soft in its taste as a mother's embrace,
and a gentleness saying as much.

To Dinner Party and Friends—

May the roof above us never fall in,
and may we friends gathered below never fall out.
Let's all put on our dancin' shoes
And wear our shamrocks green
And toast our friends both here and there
And everywhere between.

Long live the Irish, long live the cheer,
Long live our friendship, year after year!

To Birthday—

May you live as long as you want
and never want as long as you live!
May you live to be a hundred years,
with one extra year to repent!

To The Opposite Sex—
>Bless your little Irish Heart,
>and every other Irish Part!

To Wedding—
>*May you have many children*
>*and may they grow as mature in taste*
>*and healthy in color*
>*and as sought after*
>*as the contents of this glass.*

To Anniversary—
>I have known many, liked not a few;
>loved only one, I drink to you!

For a Happy Death—
>When your eyes shall be closing
>and your mouth be opening
>and your senses be slipping away;
>When your heart shall grow cold
>and your limbs be old
>God comfort your soul that day.

To A Wake—
> May every hair on your head turn into a candle
> to light your way to heaven,
> and may God and His Holy Mother
> take the harm of the years away from you.

General Blessings—
> *May you have warm words on a cold evening,*
> *a full moon on a dark night,*
> *and a smooth road all the way to your door.*

General Blessings—
To our good qualities, and they are not a few!

General Blessings—
May you have the hindsight to know
where you've been,
the foresight to know where you're going,
and the insight to know when you're going too far.

✸ SAYINGS ✸

If you're lucky enough to be Irish.... you're lucky enough.

An Irishman is never drunk as long as he can hold onto a single blade of grass and not fall off the face of the earth.

The only difference between an Irish wedding and an Irish wake is one less drunk.

Ireland is the one place on earth
that Heaven has kissed—
        with melody, mirth, and meadow and mist.

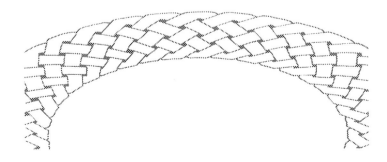

❀ IRISH PROVERBS ❀

*"The genius, wit and spirit of a nation
are discovered in its proverbs"*
—FRANCIS BACON

As with the Blessings above, these Proverbs are provided for their "pure pleasure and enjoyment." However, be creative in how you incorporate them into your celebration. These may be easier than limericks for playing charades; or they may be inscribed and decorated a la the *Book of Kells,* and hung for display in homes, classrooms and public places. Good luck with your own ideas!

❀ Youth sheds many a skin.

❀ Youth does not mind where it sets its foot.

❀ *Instinct is stronger than upbringing.*

❀ *A friend's eye is a good mirror.*

❀ Two shorten the road.

⊛ *What fills the eye fills the heart.*

⊛ Your feet will bring you to where your heart is.

⊛ *The only cure for love is marriage.*

⊛ Marriages are all happy; it's
having breakfast together that
causes all the trouble.

⊛ *Woe to him who does not
follow a good woman's advice.*

⊛ A man's work is from sun to sun,
but a woman's work is never done.

⊛ *Your son is your son until he
marries, but your daughter is your
daughter until you die.*

⊛ There are two sides to every story,
and twelve versions of a song.

⊛ It is not a secret if
it is known to three people.

⊛ *The wearer best knows*
where the shoe pinches.

⊛ *The world would not make*
a racehorse of a donkey.

⊛ A raggy colt often made a powerful horse.

⊛ It is a good horse that
draws its own cart.

⊛ *The steed does not retain its speed forever.*

⊛ *Make the fence or you*
will pay for the plunder.

⊛ Even a small thorn causes festering.

⊛ *It takes time to build castles.*

⊛ If you do not sow in the spring
you will not reap in the autumn.

⊛ There is no luck except
where there is discipline.

⚛ *The mills of God grind slowly
but they grind exceedingly fine.*

⚛ God's help is nearer than the door.

⚛ *The old pipe gives
the sweetest smoke.*

⚛ A silent mouth is sweet to hear.

⚛ A nod is as good as
a wink to a blind horse.

⚛ *A trout in the pot is better
than a salmon in the sea.*

⚛ There are finer fish in the sea
than have ever been caught.

⚛ There was never a scabby
sheep in a flock that didn't like
to have a comrade.

⚛ *If you have one pair of good soles,
it's better than two pairs of good uppers.*

Chapter Nine
BLARNEY

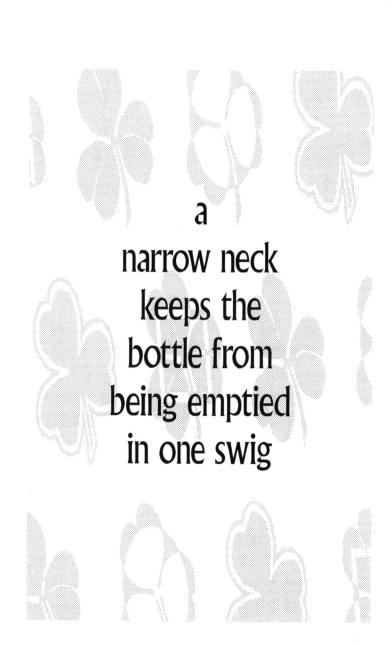

a
narrow neck
keeps the
bottle from
being emptied
in one swig

"answers to"
Irish Word Scramble

(from page 59)

SAINT PATRICK	SHILLELAGH
POTATO	CELTIC CROSS
GAELIC	PUBLIC HOUSE
PIPE	IRISH WHISKEY
LEPRECHAUN	BLARNEY STONE
POT O' GOLD	SAINT BRIGID
SHAMROCK	DRUIDS
HARP	BANSHEE
BLESSING	CLADDAGH*
RAINBOW	PEAT BOG
EMERALD ISLE	SHENANIGANS
IRISH STEW	BOOK OF KELLS

GLOSSARY OF WORDS

SAINT PATRICK:

Patron Saint of Ireland and the Irish. Many legends surround his life and his conversion of the Celtic people to Christianity. His feast day is celebrated March 17, the day of his death.

* Yes, a shenanigan it was to leave Claddagh unscrambled!

POTATO:

"Praties" were the staple of Irish diet. Also a source of poteen (yes, protein of sorts!), illicitly distilled whiskey made from potatoes. Oft labeled "St. Patrick's Pot," poteen was made, sold, or drunk in small cottages called "shebeens."

GAELIC:

The Celtic or "Irish" language, can refer to Irish speaking people.

G.K. CHESTERTON, in
"The Ballad of the White Horse," wrote—

For the great Gaels of Ireland
Are the men that God made mad,
For all their wars are merry,
And all their songs are sad.

PIPE:

Short and long-stemmed tobacco pipes commonly made of Irish clay, also symbols of Ireland.

LEPRECHAUN:

Fairy creature of Ireland, portrayed as a

bearded, wizened, wrinkled little man or dwarf, camouflaged in a green suit and cap. The name comes from the Irish *leith brog,* meaning the one-shoemaker, since he is generally seen working on a single shoe. He is a solitary figure, considered rich, and sometimes mean and spiteful, but who also delights in music and dance. Perhaps any spitefulness comes from their being relegated by the Christian religion to a mythical stature.

WILLIAM ALLINGHAM, in *"The Leprechaun: or Fairy Shoemaker,"* poetically asks—

> Do you not catch the tiny clamor,
> Busy click of an Elfin hammer,
> Voice of the Leprechaun singing shrill,
> As he merrily plies his trade?

POT O' GOLD:
The hidden treasure of every respectable leprechaun. This pot or crock is thought to be hidden, and sought to be found, at the rainbow's end.

SHAMROCK:

Bright green clover and emblem of the Irish. St. Patrick pointed to its three leafs to illustrate

the concept of the Trinity— *three persons* (leafs) in *one God* (plant).

This sentimental Irish song conveys
the specialness of the shamrock—

There's a dear little plant that grows in our Isle
'Twas St. Patrick himself sure that set it
And the sun on his labor with pleasure did smile
And with a tear from his eye oft-times wet it
It shines through the bog, through the brook, through the mireland,
And he called it the dear little Shamrock of Ireland.

HARP:

Symbol of Ireland. The gold harp of Tara emblazons the green flag of Eire and Irish coin (and the label of Guinness beer!). The old Irish harp, the "clarsach," symbolizes sorrow and joy. Harps played a part in passing on myths and legends. In one myth, the first harp was owned by the Dagda, highest of Divine Folk. He alone could draw forth its moods of joy, sorrow and repose. Envious of Dagda, the powers of cold and darkness stole the harp and hid it in their fortress. The gods of light and art were sent to rescue it. At the chilly fortress hung the sacred harp. By repeating the harp's secret name, the gods seized it back. Dagda then held a council and played upon the harp a "wail" strain to make them weep, a "smile" strain to make them joyful, and a "sleep" strain that transposed the whole council into blissful repose. (Paraphrased from *Barth*)

The Irish poet Yeats believed that beautiful old Irish tunes are in essence fairy music picked up by eavesdroppers. One such person was the blind O'Carolan, the last great Irish harpist. It is said that O'Carolan fell asleep one night upon a fairy mound, and ever after fairy tunes played on in his head.

Over the past centuries the harp and its stories have fallen silent, as reflected in this ould Irish verse put to poem by THOMAS MORE—

The Harp that once through Tara's Halls,
The soul of music shed,
Now hangs as mute on Tara's walls,
As if that soul were fled.

Today you may find the harp "played" with pipe and fiddle, tin whistle, accordion or concertina, and *bodhran and bones* (flat drum and drumstick)—as part of the Irish celebration of ceili.

BLESSING:

A prayer of luck and grace. A mixture of traditional Irish faith, wisdom, and folklore that touches on superstition and simple well-wishes. Many blessings have been adapted from the great prayer called the Breastplate of Saint Patrick.

RAINBOW:

An arching mist of light in full color spectrum. Rainbows are a common sight over the Emerald Isle after rain showers.

EMERALD ISLE:

Poetic name for Ireland, popular because of the deep green of Ireland's fields and trees.

> WILLIAM DRENNAN claimed to have coined the name in his poem *ERIN,* and so referred to her again in *Eire*—

Arm of Erin! prove strong; but be gentle as brave,
And, uplifted to strike, still be ready to save;
Nor one feeling of vengeance presume to defile
The cause, or the men, of the Emerald Isle.
When Eire first rose from the dark-swelling flood,
God blessed the green island, and saw it was good;
The Emerald of Europe, it sparkled and shone,
In the ring of the world, the most precious stone.
In her sun, in her soil, in her station thrice blest,
With her back towards Britain, her face to the west,
Eire stands proudly insular, on her steep shore,
And strikes her high harp 'mid the ocean's deep roar.

IRISH STEW:

A traditional recipe consisting of chunks of lamb, potatoes, carrots, and leeks. A variation that is "irresistibly Irish" has chunks of beef in a rich sauce made with Guinness stout beer.

SHILLELAGH:

A short club—cudgel—stick, traditionally of blackthorn or oak. Originally a "sprig" cut from the oak forest of Shillelagh, County Wicklow, the shillelagh is sometimes called the "Irish boxing glove."

Of the shillelagh it is written—

Oh! An Irishman's heart is as stout as shillelagh,
　It beats with delight to chase sorrow or woe;
　When the piper plays up, then it dances as gaily,
　And thumps with a whack to leather a foe.

CELTIC CROSS:

The classic symbol of Irish faith. It is said to represent the Christian Cross of Christ fused with the round sun, source of life and center of Celtic pagan beliefs in nature spirits.

PUBLIC HOUSE:

The full title from which the common word "pub" is derived.

IRISH WHISKEY:

Uisce beatha, water of life. This is the preferred drink of many (even Patrick) —next to Guinness stout beer.

BLARNEY STONE:

A block of limestone in Blarney Castle. Legend has it the owner of the castle used promises and flattery to save it from attackers.

Other legends invoke its magic in love.

Modern myth holds that a person who kisses this blarney stone will be given the power of sweet, persuasive, clever, convincing eloquence and flattery, the "gift of blarney." To kiss the Blarney Stone, one must climb the tower to the top of McCarthy's Castle, and lying on one's back, lean out under the turret to kiss the stone embedded in its underside.

SAINT BRIGID:

Patron Saint of Ireland, second only to Patrick, the "Mary of Gael." Brigid is renowned for her charitable deeds, miraculous acts, and courage. Inspired by Patrick, she renounced marriage and founded a monastic order for women, the most famous site of which is "Cell of the Oak" at Kildare. Many fascinating tales surround Brigid. The St. Brigid Cross, woven from rushes, is still made in Ireland today, and hung in cottages on St. Brigid's Day, February 1, to ward off harm.

DRUIDS:
Priestly cult among ancient Celts. Druids dwelt in forests and caves, giving instructions foretelling events, performing rites, and ministering justice. They held sacred the hours of midnight and noon, the oak tree, and the mistletoe.

BANSHEE:
In Irish legend, this was an old woman whose shriek and wailing (called "keening") outside a house, meant there was to be a death inside.

CLADDAGH:
An Irish design of two hands clasping the heart, denotes the entwining of true love, fidelity, and loyalty.

PEAT BOG:
Area of clay-like turf similar to the edge of swamps. From the bog, black earth is cut into bricks of peat, dried, and burned for heat and fuel.

SHENANIGANS:
Various acts of mischief or trickery commonly perpetrated by witty Irishmen, hooligans, or leprechauns!

BOOK OF KELLS:
Illuminated gospels of Celtic Christian art inscribed by monks from the monastery of Saint Columcille at Kells.

ᛏ   ᛏ   ᛏ

"Connections to"
Irish Cities & Landmarks
(from page 61)

LIMERICK. . . . . . .city of humorous poetry wrote Edward Lear

BUNRATTY CASTLE. . . . .
. . . . medieval diner dishing banquets and culture

CLIFFS OF MOHER . . . . Atlantic test for leap of faith

ARAN ISLANDS. . . fishermen wives keep tourists in stitches

GALWAY. . . . . seagals flock to see horse races in summer

CROAGH PATRICK. . . . .
. . . . .mountain Patrick croaked of climbing, by God!

KNOCK. . . . . . holy water packs a punch swears churchkeeper

DONEGAL. . . . . . ."woolen sweaters on sale" cheep the birds

RIVER SHANNON. .loughs flow down by this old mill stream

DUBLIN. . . . . "dark pool" in Gaelic, likely spilt stout

RIVER LIFFEY. . . no hay penny? a half penny will do to cross

TRINITY COLLEGE. . . . .
. . . . Father, Son & Holy Ghost are professors here

IRISH STUD FARM. . . . .
. . . . .real horses, real men, sow wild oats and foal

WATERFORD. . . . . . . hear the crystal sound of breaking glass

TIPPERARY. . . . .dairy town tipped the, er —milk bottle daily!

CORK. . . . . .St. Finbar's plug for altar wine, oft-popped

BLARNEY CASTLE. . . . .
. . . . "everybody must get stoned" coaxes Bob Dylan

COBH. . . . ."cove" in Gaelic, not "corn-on-the-stalk"

RING OF KERRY. . . . . like sheep that pass on the right?

LAKES OF KILLARNEY. . . . .
. . . . jaunting round Muckross Estate, step rightly!

SHANNON. . . . . . . .has customs for coming or going duty free

ㅣ   ㅣ   ㅣ

"A Ten Round Decision"
in the **Irish Boxing Match**
(from page 63)

Saint Patrick. . . . . Gave *Confession* to his mission in Erin

Samuel Becket. . . . . Still *Waiting For Godot*

Brendan Behan. . . . . *Borstal Boy* busted by the Brits

James Joyce. . . . . Portrayed *Ulysses* as a young man

Sean O'Casey. . . . . . His play was a real *Cock-a-Doodle Dandy*

George Bernard Shaw. . . . His *Pygmalion* created my fair lady

Jonathan Swift. . . . . Has nightmares about *Lilliputians*

John Millington Synge. . . A real *Playboy of the Western World*

Oscar Wilde. . . . . Believed in *Importance of Being Earnest*

William Butler Yeats. . . . . Wrote poetry to *Wild Swans at Coole*

CHAPTER 9
CONCLUSION

a good retreat
is better than
a bad stand

This St. Patrick's Day Festivity Book has accomplished its purpose if it has "blessed thee" with activities not only for this day, but for other occasions as well, and, also, if it has given ye a bit more knowledge of Ireland, its people, history, and culture. More could be said on Irish-American ways, and plenty more on Irish games of darts, cards, sports, horse racing, etc. But I retreat and leave you to take a stand. These "drafts" of ideas, poured out in a spirit of good will and good cheer, have tapped gaiety and gratitude. It is my prayer that these elixirs will highlight your celebration and distill fond memories in all. To this end, I personally thank you for your (dare I say) "pious" interest in St. Patrick's Day. Your comments on the celebration are most welcomed, as are your inquiries or book requests.

Please write—

Michael J. Fallon - **Educare**
1114 Pomeroy Avenue
Santa Clara, CA 95051
mjfallon@worldnet.att.net

A note of significance: it is in the spirit of St. Patrick that peace and good will extend to all people of the Emerald Isle, especially the children. For this cause, a portion of the proceeds from this book will be donated to the Irish Children's Fund, Inc. for their work for "peace in Northern Ireland through reconciliation." If you wish to make an additional donation, or desire more information, contact the ICF at their USA address:

THE IRISH CHILDREN'S FUND, INC.
47 B. West St. Charles Rd.
Villa Park, IL 60191
1 (708) 833-1910

P.S.—

The Irish toast to St. Patrick's Day, "May we all be alive and well and together this time next year," could be followed with, "Next year in Ireland!" Perhaps now is the time to plan your trip!

Whether for St. Patrick's Day or anytime, Ireland can be easily reached by air from all points in the United States and Canada. Charter flights operate from several gateways and can be booked through travel agents or direct. Getting around in Ireland is convenient, and questions of where to stay and where to go will be quickly answered with "cead mille failte." If your St. Patrick's Day celebration has you dreamy and misty-eyed for Eire, phone the Irish Tourist Board at 800-223-6470. Tell 'em "Saint Patrick sent ye!"

Erin Go Bragh!

R E S O U R C E S

BARTH, EDNA— *Shamrocks, Harps, and Shillelaghs,*
[HOUGHTON-MIFFLIN / CLARION BOOKS, New York, 1977.]

Bon Appéttit,
[May, 1996] *'An Irish Thirst...,' pages 52-56*

CANTWELL, MARY— *St. Patrick's Day*
[THOMAS Y. CROMWELL CO., New York, 1967]

FAIROS, PAT— *Irish Blessings*
[CHRONICLE BOOKS, San Francisco,1992]

FISHER, AILEEN— *Holiday Programs
for Boys and Girls,*
[PLAYS, INC., BOSTON MA, 1953 / 1970.]

FITZGIBBON, THEODORA— *A Taste of Ireland*
[HOUGHTON-MIFFLIN CO., Boston, 1969]

Ireland of the Welcomes,
[Vol. 42 No. 1, January-February 1993]
'The Place in Song'

Ireland of the Welcomes,
[Vol. 43 No. 2, March-April 1994]
'St. Patrick's Tour of Ireland' by LIAM DE PAOR
Irish Blessings,
[GREEWICH HOUSE, DIVISION OF ARLINGTON HOUSE
INC., Crown Publishers, New York, 1983]

Irish Proverbs. Illustrated by KAREN BAILY
[CHRONICLE BOOKS, San Francisco, 1986]

KAMERMAN, SYLVIA E., editor— *Fifty Plays for Holidays*
[PLAYS INC., Boston, 1969]

Laughable Limericks.
Complied by SARA & JOHN E. BREWTON
[THOMAS Y. CROMWELL COMPANY, New York, 1965]

LENISTON, FLORENCE, editor— *Popular Irish Songs*
[DOVER PUBLICATIONS, INC., New York, 1992]

MAC CON IOMAIRE, LIAM— *Ireland of the Proverb*
[MASTERS PRESS, Grand Rapids,1988]

McCARTHY, JOHN—*The Best of Irish With and Wisdom*
[THE CONTINUMM PUBLISHING CO., NEW YORK, 1987]

PARROT, E.O.—*The Penguin Book of Limericks*
[PENGUIN BOOKS LTD., LONDON, 1983]

REILLY, ROBERT T.—*Irish Saints*
[AVENEL BOOKS, CROWN PUBLISHERS INC.,
New York, 1964]

SPAULDING, HENRY D.—*Joys of Irish Humor*
[JONATHON DAVID PUBLISHERS INC.,
Middle Village NY, 1978 / 1989.]

World Book Encyclopedia
[VOL. 12, FEILD ENTERPRISES
EDUCATIONAL CORPORATION 1977]
'Ireland and Related Articles'

May all the joy
that echoes through
a happy Irish song,
and all the luck
the shamrock brings
be yours the whole year long,
May you have blessings,
pleasures and friends
to gladden all life's way,
and may St. Patrick smile on you
today and every day.

May the road rise up to meet you

May the wind be ever at your back

May the sun shine warm upon your face

The rain fall soft upon your fields

And until we meet again

May God hold you in the palm of His hand.

An Old Irish Verse

Michael James Fallon
*is an educator who has
spent time researching St.
Patrick and Irish culture,
including trips to Ireland.
He developed this book after
two decades of collecting
lore and tradition as well as
orchestrating celebrations
in his family, classrooms,
and for community
organizations.
Mr. Fallon was raised in
Ohio and now resides
with his family in
Santa Clara,
California.*

Order or Tour

The Definitive
St. Patrick's Day
Festivity Book

at

www.serve.com/iaf/mar17.html

Educare
408-247-9940 or 1-888-MARCH17

MJF dba Educare
Santa Clara, California
1997